SEMEIA 78

READING THE BIBLE AS WOMEN: PERSPECTIVES FROM AFRICA, ASIA, AND LATIN AMERICA

Editor: Phyllis A. Bird

Guest Editors: Katharine Doob Sakenfeld, and Sharon H. Ringe

Editorial Consultants:
Seung Ai Yang
Leticia Guardiola-Sáenz
Dora Rudo Mbuwayesango

SEMEIA 78

ISSN 0095-571X
ISBN 1-58983-185-3

Printed in the United States of America
on acid-free paper

CONTENTS

RESPONSES

CONTRIBUTORS TO THIS ISSUE

Phyllis A. Bird
Garrett-Evangelical Theological
Seminary
2121 Sheridan Road
Evanston, IL 60201
(847) 866-3976
e-mail: p-bird@nwu.edu

Ahida Cama-Calderón
Lutheran Theological School
at Chicago
1100 East 55th Street
Chicago, IL 60615
(773) 363-2436
e-mail: Acamacalde@aol.com

Julie Li-Chuan Chu
No. 56-1, Sec. 1, Han-Kou Rd.
407 Taichung
TAIWAN
Fax: 886-4-326-0049

Musa W. Dube
University of Botswana
BOTSWANA
e-mail: dubemw@noka.ub.bw

Mercedes García Bachmann
Lutheran Theological School
at Chicago
1100 East 55th Street
Chicago, IL 60615
(773) 493-5473
e-mail: mgarciab@mcs.net

Leticia Guardiola-Sáenz
1917 Adelicia St.
Nashville, TN 37212
(615) 329-0344
e-mail: l.a.guardiola@vanderbilt.edu

Beverley G. Haddad
School of Theology
University of Natal
Private Bag X01
Scottsville 3209
Pietermaritzburg
SOUTH AFRICA
e-mail: haddad@theology.unp.ac.za

Jean K. Kim
145 50th Ave. N.
Nashville, TN 37209
(615) 385-2508
jean.k.kim@vanderbilt.edu

Madipoane Masenya
University of South Africa
P.O. Box 2805
0700 Pietersburg
SOUTH AFRICA
e-mail: masenmj@alpha.unisa.ac.za

Dora Rudo Mbuwayesango
Hood Theological Seminary
800 W. Thomas St.
Salisbury, NC 28144
(708) 638-5434
e-mail: 102624.245@compuserve.com

Monica Jyotsna Melanchthon
Gurukul Lutheran Theological
College
94 Purasawalkam High Road
Kellys, Chennai 600 010
INDIA
Fax: 91-44-642-1870

Elna Mouton
Department of Biblical and Religion
Studies
University of Port Elizabeth
P.O. Box 1600
Port Elizabeth 6000
SOUTH AFRICA
e-mail: bsaaem@upe.ac.za

Ranjini Rebera
38 Moos Lane
Bergenfeld, NJ 07621
(201) 384-3901
reb@worldnet.att.net

Sharon H. Ringe
Wesley Theological Seminary
4500 Massachusetts Ave. NW
Washington, DC 20016
(202) 885-8643
e-mail: ringesh@aol.com

Katharine Doob Sakenfeld
Princeton Theological Seminary
P.O. Box 821
Princeton, NJ 08542-0803
(609) 497-7818
e-mail:
katharine.sakenfeld@ptsem.edu

Malika A. Sibeko
Institute for the Study of the Bible
School of Theology
University of Natal
Private Bag X01
Scottsville 3209
Pietermaritzburg
SOUTH AFRICA
e-mail: sibekoM@theology.unp.ac.za

Antoinette Clark Wire
2617 LeConte
Berkeley, CA 94709
(415) 258-6572

Seung Ai Yang
St. Paul Seminary School
of Divinity
2260 Summit Avenue
St. Paul, MN 55105-1094
(651) 962-5061
e-mail: sayang@stthomas.edu

Yani (Yeon Hee) Yoo
P.O. Box 1397
Oliverbridge, NY 12461
(212) 678-9089
e-mail: yy60@columbia.edu

INTRODUCTION

Phyllis A. Bird, Katharine Doob Sakenfeld, and Sharon H. Ringe

The essays in this volume have no common theme, method, or hermeneutic. What unites them is the gender and social location of their authors, which have served to exclude them from the discourse of North American biblical scholarship and, more generally, from the guild of professional biblical interpreters. As women from cultures that have traditionally reserved academic and clerical professions to males, these authors speak from and about the boundaries that mark their lives as women and as biblical interpreters. They have come to voice in these pages by diverse paths and with diverse aims. They employ a variety of tools and address a variety of audiences. In this volume, however, they address "us"—North American biblical scholars and literary critics.[1] Through direct and indirect discourse they address us across the boundaries that have previously excluded them. The editors, North American women with varying degrees of experience in the world of the authors, present these essays in the conviction that they have something essential to contribute to our own work as biblical scholars and teachers.

We recognize the problematic nature of our efforts to present the work of women from the Two-Thirds World, as perpetuating patterns of domination and subordination that we wish to challenge. After considering various options, however, we decided that we must take responsibility for the project that we had conceived and initiated—with the hope that future works of biblical interpretation by women from Africa, Asia, and Latin America will not need the intermediation of North American biblical scholars—but will command dialogue with them. We have felt an obligation as members of the dominant culture to expose the limits of our own horizons and the biases of our own training and work. Closed doors must normally be opened from the inside—though once opened, they invite passage in both directions.

---

1 We are cognizant and appreciative of *Semeia's* wider audience. We nevertheless recognize that it is primarily an organ of the North American guild of biblical scholars, whose attempts at fostering international dialogue are still grounded in North American institutional and economic realitites. A more comprehensive designation of the readership may be desirable, but in the interests of a manageable expression we have opted for this oversimplification.

Consultation and collaboration with women from Africa, Asia, and Latin America have been integral to every stage of the conception and production of this volume, from the initial Consultation held at the SBL Annual Meeting in Chicago (1994) to the final selection of essays and editorial advice to contributors. Rather than trying to find a single woman from the Two-Thirds World to serve as a co-editor and bear the burden of representing three immensely diverse continents, we opted for a board of three Editorial Consultants. In this manner we were able to insure that every essay submitted for consideration was assessed by at least one reader from the Two-Thirds World, and where possible by someone with shared interests, experience, or expertise. The three Consultants provided invaluable assistance in their astute critiques and helpful comments and played a decisive role in the shape of this volume.

The volume was born of a growing recognition that something was missing in the new attention to readers and the role of culture and social location in biblical interpretation. In 1990 the Bible in Africa, Asia, and Latin America Group was established in the Society of Biblical Literature with the aim of fostering interchange between biblical scholars of North America and their colleagues in Africa, Asia, and Latin America (hereafter AALA).[2] In directing attention to regions and cultures peripheral to those in which biblical scholarship had developed as an academic discipline, it acknowledged the growing significance of this world beyond its borders—and the growing presence of members from that world in its midst. It provided a venue for "voices from the margins," and in so doing challenged the notions of "center" and "margins." Discussion within the Group also problematized a number of practices or assumptions of Western bibilical scholarship, including the separation of academic and theological interpretation and the relationship of trained to untrained readers.

What the Group failed to problematize in its first years, however, was the overwhelmingly male cast of participants from AALA. A move to address this issue in its final year (1995)[3] resulted in a double session devoted entirely to papers by women from AALA. This move was stimulated by the 1995 centennial of Elizabeth Cady Stanton's *Woman's Bible* and the request by the SBL

---

2 This unwieldy list of continents corresponds closely, but not completely, to the designations, "Third World"—or "Two-Thirds World"—and "Southern Hemisphere/Tier." While all imply contrasts of an historical, economic, and cultural nature, the naming of the regions signals an intention to honor the distinctness of each and invite attention to internal diversity as well. At the same time, uniting the regions in a single group signals an interest in exploring common issues, such as the colonial legacy that has left a particularly heavy stamp on bibical interpretation. We have adopted the expression "Two-Thirds World" as a collective designation where commonalities or contrasts with the North Atlantic world are in view, recognizing that no collective term is fully adequate and that all express a point of view, and a history, that cannot be neutralized.

3 The Group, which had an initial term of five years, has been continued as a Section.

Program Committee for all program units to honor the occasion by special attention to women and women's issues. Twelve women from ten countries presented papers in what proved to be the first assembly of women biblical scholars from AALA held anywhere in the world. The papers from that session provided the basis for the selected and expanded collection presented here.

The process of assembling and editing these essays has been a long one, with many obstacles. We have knocked on many doors that did not open or opened only to blank stares: "no women here," "no women biblical scholars." Announcements, letters, and phone calls to SBL colleagues and contacts in AALA yielded a few names, but mostly silence. At the same time papers and inquiries arrived from "nowhere," through contacts we could not trace, as word of the project spread through an invisible network of women. As we planned for the 1995 session, we realized that many of the women whom we would like to include in the program would be unable to attend the session in Philadelphia, and others would require special assistance, and intervention, in order to participate. Of the few women from AALA trained, or training, in biblical studies, few held academic positions or were employed by institutions that would support travel to the meeting, and those who did have academic positions were typically in the lowest ranks. The core group would have to be drawn from women presently studying or employed in the U.S. We were intent, nevertheless, on assisting any woman from overseas whose paper was accepted and were finally able, with aid from the SBL, to bring four women from Nicaragua, Kenya, and South Africa to the meeting. Many potential contributors were unable to speak in that forum, however, for reasons of language, cost, timing, and travel restrictions. Recognizing these limits, we envisioned a publication that would open the door to a wider range of contributors and reach a larger audience. With the encouragement of the *Semeia* editorial board, we began to prepare for this edition, even as we planned the 1995 meeting.

The fact that this first assembly of women biblical scholars from AALA took place in Philadelphia, rather than in the Two-Thirds World, is a reminder of the circumstances under which women from these regions enter the world of biblical scholarship. It remains in large measure "foreign turf," controlled by institutions/guilds, ideologies, and rules of participation that are alien to the culture of these participants. At the same time, however, a growing circle of women theologians has come into being in the Two-Thirds World, linked to a world-wide network of women theologians and uniting women with varying types and degrees of theological training in attention to issues of particular concern to women in their regions. It is in these associations that women's biblical interpretation in AALA is primarily centered.

While academic study of the Bible remains largely an alien enterprise for women of AALA, the Bible itself has played a central and determining role in most of their lives—at least among women raised in Christian traditions, or in cultures influenced by Christian missions—which includes most of the former colonial world. The Bible in this world is both a primary theological source, providing inspiration and guidance, and a source of rules and models that govern, and restrict, women's lives. In this world women commonly meet for Bible study in women's groups, led either by a lay woman or a male pastor, and even women who are unable to read know the Bible—as friend and foe. Yet women whose lives are subjected to the authority of the Bible have generally been denied authority to interpret it for themselves. It is not surprising then that when invited to contribute essays on texts of their own choosing, all chose texts in which women appear—texts that had been used against them or other women in their culture, or texts that suggested liberating possibilities for women. The luxury, or the aberration/irresponsibility, of "disinterested" scholarship is rejected by all of these contributors, who bring the silent and silenced women of their homelands into their interpretation. This becomes clear as we briefly consider each of the authors and their research interests.

Musa W. Dube is a citizen of Botswana, where she is New Testament Lecturer in the University of Botswana. Her main interest is in the use and impact of biblical texts in modern and contemporary times. Her research interests are in post-colonial studies, African folktales and storytelling, and feminist theories and theologies. She is co-editor editor of *Semeia* 73: *"Reading With": African Overtures* and author of "Reading for Decolonization (Jn 4:1–42)" in *Semeia* 75.

Dora Rudo Mbuwayesango received her B.A. in Religious Studies from the University of Zimbabwe in Harare and an M.T.S. from Harvard Divinity School. She has recently completed a Ph.D. dissertation at Emory University on "The Defense of Zion and the House of David: Isaiah 36–39 in the Context of Isaiah 1–39" and is currently Instructor of Old Testament/Hebrew Bible at Hood Theological Seminary in Salisbury, North Carolina. Her research interests focus on viewing the Hebrew people from the perspective of African cultures and on the role of the Hebrew Bible in challenging or perpetuating the oppression of women in patriarchal societies. A current project on "The Exodus and Women" draws on Jewish feminist adaptations of the Haggadah as a model for African and African American women "to celebrate women's roles in liberation events as well as to highlight their present concerns." Additional projects include a study of women as political and social "objects" in Judges 19–21, viewed from a cultural perspective, and post-apartheid readings of Joshua 1–6 and portions of Deuteronomy.

Yani (Yeon Hee) Yoo grew up in Korea under the dictatorial governments that followed the Korean War. Responding to the revivals of Christianity, she entered the Methodist Theological Seminary in Seoul, where she fell in love with the Bible. She is currently a Ph.D. candidate in Old Testament at

Union Theological Seminary in New York and sees her "lifetime homework" as reading the Bible from Asian women's experience. She has served as an education director in Methodist churches in Korea and the U.S. and was recently ordained in the New York Annual Conference of the United Methodist Church. She is the author of several articles and poems and translator of Phyllis Trible's *God and the Rhetoric of Sexuality* and Jacob Meyers' *I Chronicles* into Korean.

Julie Li-Chuan Chu was born in Taiwan of parents from mainland China. Following studies in journalism and English at the National Taiwan Normal University, she was a high school English teacher before embarking on theological studies. She has an M.Div. from Taiwan Theological Seminary (Presbyterian Church of Taiwan) and an M.Th. in biblical studies from the South East Asia Graduate School of Theology. Since 1994 she has served with her husband as co-pastor of Presbyterian churches in Taiwan. She has translated several books into Chinese, including the *Layman Commentary—The Book of Luke;* Letty M. Russell, *The Liberating Word;* Barbara J. MacHaffie, *Her Story;* and Pamela Young, *Feminist Theology.*

Madipoane Masenya (ngwana' Mphahlele) is a South African of Northern Sotho origin who is currently a Lecturer in the Department of Old Testament at the University of South Africa. Her interest in biblical interpretation from an African–South African perspective resulted in a master's dissertation contextualizing selected Hebrew proverbs in a Northern Sotho setting. Her subsequent work has been oriented towards women's issues in interpretation, particularly the need for liberationist readings of the Bible by African-South African women. She has published several articles on this subject. Her doctoral dissertation for the University of South Africa was on "Proverbs 31: 10–31 in a South African Context: A Bosadi (Womanhood) Perspective."

Leticia Guardiola-Sáenz was born in the Mexican border-town of Reynosa in a bicultural context that has continued to influence her life and work. She holds degrees in accounting and Spanish literature from the Tecnologico de Monterrey as well as an M.A. in theology and ethics and an M.Div. from Northern Baptist Theological Seminary in Lombard, Illinois. She is currently a doctoral student in New Testament at Vanderbilt University, with a dissertation project entitled "The Characterization of Jesus in the Gospel of John: Hybridity and Survival." Her interests include Johannine studies, Cultural Studies, Hispanic Feminist Hermeneutics, and postcolonial theory.

Malika A. Sibeko is a South African, who describes herself as born of a Christian family and a survivor of a patriarchal society, both in the church and the family. She is an ordained minister of the Methodist Church of Southern Africa and served the Methodist Church in Thaba-Nehu for three years. A graduate of the Federal Theological Seminary, she has a B.Th. and M.A. from the University of Natal in Pietermaritzburg. She is currently Coordinator of the Institute for the Study of the Bible, an institute of the School of

Theology at the University of Natal which operates as an interface between the University and the community/church. She also serves as a Residence Life Officer in one of the Residences at the University of Natal.

Beverley G. Haddad is an Anglican priest with a degree from St. Paul's Theological Seminary in Grahamstown, South Africa, who is currently completing doctoral studies at the University of Natal. Her research interest in the interface between gender, community development, and theology is focused on the "working theologies of survival" of marginalized black South African women. She teaches in the masters program in Leadership and Development at the School of Theology and works part-time in a Zulu-speaking semi-rural Anglican congregation on the outskirts of Pietermaritzburg. Originally trained as a social worker at the University of the Witwatersrand, she earned an M.A. in Development Studies at the University of the Western Cape, based on her experience in marginalized communities around Cape Town. She is the author of "En-gendering a Theology of Development: Raising Some Preliminary Issues," in *Archbishop Tutu: Prophetic Witness in South Africa* (eds. L. Hulley, L. Kretzschmar, L. Pato; 1996) and edited "En-gendering Theology: South African voices," *Bulletin for Contextual Theology in South and Southern Africa* 4 (2), 1997.

Ranjini Rebera is an Australian of Sri Lankan origin, currently residing in the U.S. A member of the Uniting Church of Australia, she has been active in her own church and in ecumenical circles in Asia and the Pacific as a lecturer, workshop leader, and author. She is presently engaged in free-lance work as a Consultant in Communication and Gender, designing and facilitating workshops to equip women as leaders in church and society and educating in creative, feminist Bible study methods. Her many publications include the following: *Affirming Difference, Celebrating Wholeness—A Partnership of Equals* (editor and contributor; Christian Council of Asia, 1995); *A Search for Symbols: An Asian Experiment* (author; CCA, 1990); *We Cannot Dream Alone: A Story of Women in Development* (editor; World Council of Churches, 1990).

Jean K. Kim earned a B.S. and M.S. in chemistry from Ewha Womans University and Sogang Graduate School, respectively, and worked at the Korean Advanced Institute of Science and Technology as a science researcher before entering Ewha Graduate School in 1984 to study theology. After receiving her M.A. in New Testament, she continued her studies at Boston University School of Theology and Vanderbilt University, where she is currently pursuing a Ph.D. in New Testament. Her commitment to "give silent women characters a chance to speak rather than following the traditional biblical interpretation" arises from her pastoral experience in a Korean-American church located near a military base (reflected in her interpretation of John 4) and from the unhappy married life of her mother, who was forced to marry to avoid being kidnapped by Japanese soldiers as a comfort woman.

She is the author of "An Asian Interpretation of Phil 2:6–11," in *Marking Boundaries: Essays in/on Feminist Theological Hermeneutics*, forthcoming.

Elna Mouton is an Afrikaans speaking South African who is currently senior lecturer in New Testament in the Department of Biblical and Religion Studies at the University of Port Elizabeth, South Africa. She has been constantly exposed to the pragmatic dimensions and consequences of biblical interpretation in the most diverse situations: a "missionary" setting in the Xhosa-speaking regions of the Transkei and interdenominational hospital and industrial ministry, the confines of the traditional and male-dominated Dutch Reformed Church, the academic environment of a university, and a congregation where she serves as elder with its challenge to read with "ordinary readers." She studied at the universities of Stellenbosch, Port Elizabeth, and the Western Cape, obtaining her D.Th. from the latter with an ethical reading of the Epistle to the Ephesians. She has published in various theological journals and has contributed to edited volumes on New Testament hermeneutics, rhetoric, the role of women in the Bible and the church, and the transformative potential of the Bible as a resource for Christian ethos and ethics.

All of the women who speak in these pages speak out of an experience of boundary crossings. Those who employ the methodological and conceptual tools of Western biblical scholarship move between two worlds as they attempt to bring their cultural experience to their scholarship and as they attempt to relate their scholarship to the world in which they reside or from which they have come. Some speak from distant lands, and some speak from our midst, as students and colleagues in our own institutions, but all speak in some sense as bi-cultural persons. That is true not only for those who adopt Western critical methods, but also for those who reject an academic approach or who chose to emphasize the role of the reader and indigenous or popular modes of interpretation. The very enterprise in which they are engaged has come, like the Bible itself, from abroad. Its colonial past and missionary origins linger even as attempts are made to re-form it. Moreover the culture itself bears indelible marks of the Western world, in neo-colonial as well as colonial legacies. Thus all of the essays in this volume speak from or about boundaries, internal and external, and all show in one way or another the peculiar ways in which these boundaries impact women.

None of these essays should be understood as "representative" of interpretation in a particular country or culture. All are individual responses. They do give a picture, however, of the variety of approaches and presuppositions being used today by women in and from AALA, including those who are claiming a place at the table of scholarly discourse previously set in and by the West. All are concerned in one way or another with finding a language appropriate to the particular bicultural, or multicultural, context in which they find themselves. Thus some employ categories of post-colonial critique, while others adopt liberationist approaches. Some use the language of feminist or womanist analysis, while others derive their key terms and categories of analysis from their own culture and history. Although the influence of western feminist scholarship may be seen in all of the essays, each author has appropriated it in a different way. Finally, the essays exhibit different hermeneutical presuppositions and aims and espouse different strategies for overcoming the needs they identify, as the respondents have pointed out, among other things.

Antoinette Clark Wire was born in China of missionary parents and began high school in Shanghai. Returning to California with her parents, she continued her education at Pomona College and Yale Divinty School (B.D.) before earning a Ph.D. in New Testament at Claremont Graduate School. She is Professor of New Testament at San Francisco Theological Seminary and the Graduate Theological Union, where her current research focuses on early Jewish oral traditions with an interest in who first told the stories about Jesus. Recent publications include *The Corinthian Women Prophets: A Reconstruction Through Paul's Rhetoric* (Fortress, 1990) and articles on the miracle stories of the Gospel traditions, the sayings of Jesus, gender roles in the Matthean community, and the theology of Paul. In the last four years she has been conducting research in China on oral songs created in rural churches, often by non-literate women. She has also contributed an article on "Chinese Biblical Interpretation Since Mid-Century" (*Biblical Interpretation* 4 [1996] 101–23).

Monica Jyotsna Melanchthon is Associate Professor of Old Testament at Gurukul Lutheran Theological College and Research Institute in Chennai (Madras), India, where she also teaches a course on "Women and the Bible" in the Department of Women's Studies. She has theological degrees from United Theological College, Bangalore (B.D.), and the Lutheran School of Theology at Chicago (Th.D.). Since returning to India, she has become involved in conversations about the Dalit reality and Dalit theology, concerned with the continuing influence of the caste system within the church, as well as the larger society. She sees an urgent need for a more adequate analysis of the interconnections between caste, sex, and economic and political domination. As one of a very small number of women with advanced training in biblical studies (two in the Serampore affiliated colleges), she also recognizes a particular need to contribute to biblical hermeneutics and interpretation drawing upon women's gender-specific experiences and the Indian culture. She is currently working on two papers on "Indian Feminist Hermeneutics" and "Female Sexuality and the Indian Culture."

Ahida Cama-Calderón was born in Peru, where she completed her B.A. in Theology from the Facultad de Teología Pontifica y Civil in Lima (the oldest university in Latin America, which only opened to lay persons in 1983). She has an M.A., with a specialization in Old Testament, from the Catholic

Theological Union and is currently enrolled in the Ph.D. program at the Lutheran School of Theology at Chicago, where she hopes to be the first Peruvian Catholic lay woman to receive a doctorate in theology. Motivated by a sense of "joyful responsibility" towards her people, she has focused her studies in the area of biblical hermeneutics. She hopes to contribute through her academic research and teaching to find new or better ways to articulate the biblical message in order to empower the voiceless people of Latin America, especially the women, and uphold their dignity.

Mercedes García Bachmann was born and raised in Argentina, where she studied theology at ISEDET, the ecumenical Protestant seminary in Buenos Aires. Ordained a pastor in the Lutheran Church of Argentina, she served for eight years in four different parishes before coming to the US for doctoral studies at the Lutheran School of Theology at Chicago. She is currently writing her dissertation on female slaves in the Deuteronomistic History and expects to return to ISEDET to teach upon completion of her degree. Her experience working with base communities in Buenos Aires has convinced her that the Bible should be "given back to the people" and has given her a commitment to build bridges to lay persons in her own interpretation and in the training of pastors. She is also concerned to bring a female dimension to the dominant liberation theology of Latin America, which remains "a very male thing."

Though united by no common theme, method, or hermeneutic, these essays do exhibit two common features that suggest need and direction for dialogue with Western readers: (1) All treat a "Christian" Bible, interpreted from within a history of Christian interpretation that is further stamped with a missionizing imprint. This history has not only resulted in the exclusion of women from clerically dominated biblical scholarship. It has also limited interchange with Jewish biblical scholars and Jewish traditions of interpretation—while focusing attention on the encounter with indigenous religious and cultural traditions. (2) All bring a moral demand to the task of biblical interpretation. Whether it reflects AALA tradition, which locates Biblical scholarship within the context of Christian education/ministry, or arises from a concern with the harmful legacy of colonial interpretation, an ethical dimension is apparent in all of the essays. In this respect they challenge North American and Western European readers to examine their own presuppositions and to consider the relationship of the Bible as an object of academic study to the Bible as a document of living faiths and a continuing cultural and religious force.

Toward a Post-Colonial Feminist Interpretation of the Bible

Musa W. Dube
University of Botswana

ABSTRACT

This paper holds that historical imperialisms and the role of Christian texts necessitates a post-colonial feminist biblical interpretation. It holds that Christian texts point beyond their origin, inviting their readers to act them out in history and cross-culturally. Hence, the paper proposes a post-colonial feminist reading strategy that strives to understand how the ideology of various ancient imperial settings informed biblical texts; that scrutinizes the power relations propounded by mission texts in their constructions of different cultures and people; that takes up an open space as a framework of reading for decolonization and liberating interdependence between women of different cultures in the world.

Introduction

To read the Bible as a Motswana African woman is to read a Western book. For many years, I have known that "biblical Christian believers" refers to the white Western believers while "pagans" refers to all non-Christian Africans.[1] I have related well to Matthew 23 and the "foolish Galatians" in Gal 3:1, not reading Galatians and Pharisees as static historical persons but as a reference to all those who are not Christians. The rebuttal of the Pharisees in Matthew 23 has carried a painful fascination for me, for what I heard from this passage was not an old first-century story, but a familiar drama of nineteenth-twentieth century imperialist history upon all non-Christian Africans.

What may seem to be a gross misreading and mistaken identities of biblical characters can be contested. Some may link it to the orality of my background. Yet oral societies can read paintings. The image of Jesus was and still

---

[1] I do not consent to the use of "Africa" insofar as it implies a uniform people. My reading is representative of neither Africa nor of Botswana, my country. Africa is too large and diverse to be represented by one person's view. I am using this category insofar as I find it heavily imposed on me by the First World and because it has come to be representative of our common oppression.

is a blue-eyed, blonde, white male, whose benevolent face, along with the
likewise white faces of his disciples, still graces our churches today. The
image of Mary the mother of Jesus was and is a white woman.[2] The devil
was, of course, a black, horned man (I do not know what color he is these
days). Heaven was cast in the Western terrain, with a riotous fusion of all
Western seasons in one painting. With all these images, my misreading and
mistaken identities go beyond the orality of my African background. Un-
doubtedly, this reading grid has a historical base, which, to my surprise, has
resisted erosion from my many years of biblical studies.

This exposition highlights that different readers act out the biblical story
at different times in history. The Western imperial readers of the nineteenth
and twentieth centuries wrote themselves into the text and characterized
non-Christians as their pagan counterparts in order to validate the latter's
subjugation. Recently, a wide range of readers, from textual ones to flesh and
blood ones, have featured in biblical interpretation. However, biblical interpretation has yet to integrate various historical biblical readers from different
points in the Christian history of the last nineteen hundred and ninety-six
years. In short, the question of how different flesh and blood readers have
acted out the biblical story in history, and how their act illumines some
meaning of the text needs to be integrated into the academic biblical studies.

The biblical story itself invites its readers to identify with it and to act
it out in history. In John 20:21, for example, the resurrected Christ says, "As
my Father sent me so I send you." Encapsulated in this sending is transference of power from Jesus to his disciples. The transference is a call to his
hearers, readers, and believers to act out his story with almost the same
authority that has characterized the Johannine Jesus. Furthermore, this transference of power, at least as it stands in the gospels (Matt 28:18–20/Lk 24:
46–47) suggests that the biblical story is an unfinished story: it invites its
own continuation in history; it resists the covers of our Bibles and writes
itself on the pages of the earth. On these grounds, it is legitimate to hold that
various biblical reader-actors, from different moments in history, should il-
lumine the meaning and implications of the text for us.

Biblical scholars have in fact highlighted that the text, as we have it, already represents a drama of believers. What the narrative presents as Jesus
speaking with his disciples represents the act of the first- and second-century
believers. Analyzing John's text, Louis Martyn has termed this phenomenon
a "two-level drama." Martyn points out that this drama did not end with
Jesus' departure or composition of the texts; rather, it continues in the person
of the paraclete, operating through the believers. Martyn holds that "in order
for the paraclete to create the two-level drama, he must look not only like
Jesus, but also like the Christian witness who is Jesus' double in that drama"

---

2 As the new African American Bible highlights, these images are still being contested.

(148). Consequently, it seems to me that to insist on dwelling on one historical time in this biblical drama, ignoring the continuing character of the story, is to do injustice to that very text.

Given that I come from a historical experience of the Bible functioning as an imperialist text, I know that the biblical story is a story that is acted out in history. I have, therefore, journeyed with some sense of injustice and emptiness in my academic biblical studies, where the Bible became an antiqued text, firmly contextualized in ancient times. As a biblical student, I wrestled with issues behind or in front of the text, and, sometimes, I dealt with the first three centuries. In short, I found academic biblical interpretation divorced from its historical reader-actors of the nineteenth and twentieth centuries. The approach bracketed my questions and my experience.

To be sure, this approach of situating biblical studies in ancient times has facilitated many liberating and helpful discoveries for me. For a start, it was liberating to know that biblical texts are not Anglo-Saxon books, but Jewish texts. It was also helpful to know that far from being pure (as the modern colonial Christian agents claimed), early Christianity borrowed from the non-Christian cultures of its origin. Nevertheless, I have discovered that the privileging of the ancient historical setting in the academic interpretation of the Bible is a powerful tool that divorces my experience and my questions from the field. By privileging the ancient history in biblical interpretation, the biblical texts are perfectly shielded from its various historical reader-actors. The question of confronting the imperialist manifestation of the text is neatly bracketed. However, as Ulrich Luz points out, biblical "texts have power and cannot be separated from their consequences," and, as he further notes, "Christianity as we all know it, is far from a history of loving your enemies."[3] For me to read the Bible as an African woman and from my experience, therefore, is to be inevitably involved with the historical events of imperialism. Indeed, to read the Bible as an African is to take a perilous journey, a sinister journey, that spins one back to connect with dangerous memories of slavery,[4] colonialism, apartheid, and neo-colonialism. To read the Bible as an African is to relive the painful equation of Christianity with civilization, paganism with savagery.

Luckily, early feminist readers insisted on women's experience as a valid interpretive framework.[5] My African experience has taught me that the biblical characters shift and change with time so that what were "foolish Galatians" (Gal 3:1) may be "Savage Africans," in one context and time, and

---

3 Luz (33) points to such atrocities as the Holocaust and links it with the interpretation of the biblical text.

4 See Katie Cannon on the Christian justification of the enslavement of Africans.

5 Although the category of feminist "experience" is being correctly problematized, it empowered many of us to voice our perspectives where the traditional approach insisted on neutral and disinterested methods of reading.

something else in another; moreover, that such labels have adverse impact upon those tagged with them. My experience has taught me that a written book does not only belong to its authors—it also belongs to its readers and users;[6] and that the history of the biblical story is not limited to the first three centuries; hence, the selection of one particular historical period as the prime reference for determining textual meaning in biblical studies is not innocent.[7] I am historically situated within this framework of facts and experiences. I, therefore, read the Bible as a black Motswana woman from the region of Southern Africa, a student of religion, a survivor of colonialism, who lives in a *luta continua* (a continuous struggle) against neo-colonialism. The latter refers to "the creation of a single international (global) financial or capital market," which is impoverishing most Two-Thirds World countries with huge debts (Lind: 31). My analysis is both feminist and post-colonial.

Post-colonial, as used here, is a literary technical term defining the setting, the use, and the classification of texts.[8] In terms of setting, it covers the period beginning with the arrival and occupation of an imperial power, the struggle against it, independence, and post-independence—a continuity which remains valid with the persistence of imperial domination (Ashcroft, Griffiths, and Tiffin: 2). Further, as Homi Bhabha (4) points out, post-colonial does not only define sequentiality or polarity between colonialism and independence; rather, it is a "gesture to the beyond" that seeks to "transform the present into an expanded and ex-centric site of experience and empowerment." Put differently, post-colonial is not a discourse of historical accusations, but a committed search and struggle for decolonization and liberation of the oppressed. In terms of classification, it refers to a complex collection of texts that are brought, born, and used in imperial settings, to legitimate, resist, or collaborate with imperialism. While this definition is an umbrella term that includes the texts of the colonizer and the colonized, the phrase "colonial discourse" is also used to distinguish the former from the latter (Chrisman and Williams: 5). As an umbrella term, a post-colonial approach is best understood as a complex myriad of methods and theories which study a wide range of texts and their participation in the making or subversion of imperialism.

Although colonizing texts are mainly written by the colonizer, they also rise from the colonized. Depending on different interest groups and stages of imperial domination, the colonized can condone its oppressors, cooperate with them, or totally reject them. Since imperialism actively adopts structural

---

6 In fact, current reading theories that insist on the reader as the maker of meaning support my assertion.

7 Tolbert (1990:5–23) contests this dwelling on "purer origins" by pointing out that it treats those who do not share this history as somehow less important.

8 I am grateful to Fernando Segovia for introducing me to post-colonial theories.

strategies of assimilation or colonizing the mind, collaboration among some circles of the colonized is unavoidable. The imperialist strategy of "control-at-a-distance" (Blaut: 70), for instance, engages some local groups (usually the upper class) to become its ruling representatives, and this conceals the face of the imperial oppressor among the colonized. Revolting local groups, in turn, come to fight the collaborating group but, sometimes, they also come to compete for the attention of the oppressor amongst themselves. The enemy and its opponents are thus fully embodied within the colonized nation, a fact that is usually reflected in the wide range of texts produced in such settings.

Post-colonial theoretical frameworks were mainly developed from the analysis of nineteenth and twentieth century literature, upon the realization that texts were powerful tools for either buttressing or counteracting imperial powers. Given that imperialism has been a recurring phenomenon in the history of the world, post-colonial applicability to various other classical texts in the human history is legitimate. Its application should, indeed, open new ways to understand most of the canonized classical texts, as to how they may reflect imperial values of their origins, and how they have functioned in various empires that have risen and fallen in history.

Imperialism, as used here, describes the tendencies of metropolitan centers to impose their images, ideas, religions, economic structures, and political control in foreign lands, (Said: 9–13). Colonialism is a political manifestation of imperialism when it includes geographical control. Imperialism, however, does not always include colonialism, nor does it end with independence. The current neo-colonialism/globalization highlights that imperialism does not have to include geographical possession.

In view of the fact that Christian biblical religion has been "unique in its imperial sponsorship" (Meeks: 1), in ancient and current times and over different people and different places, the Bible is also a colonizing text: it has repeatedly authorized the subjugation of foreign nations and lands. Further, in view of the fact that the New Testament and many other Hebrew Bible books were born in imperialist settings, they are post-colonial books. On these grounds, I shall briefly expound on reading the Bible from a post-colonial literary perspective. In particular, I read it from my historical background as an imperial/colonial text. Then, I shall explore the intersection and implications of post-colonial and feminist reading in biblical studies. In my conclusion, I shall propose that in the post-colonial era feminist biblical readers must also become decolonizing readers.

WHAT IS A POST-COLONIAL READING OF TEXTS?

Amongst its many methods, a post-colonial reading may analyze the literary constructions of colonizing texts and how they function to justify imperialism. The analysis may focus on the construction of characters, geography, travelers, gender constructions, and unspoken intentions to highlight how these work in justifying the domination of one by another. Usually, these narrative texts construct both the colonizer and the colonized to accept the legitimacy of their respective positions. Post-colonial literary analysis, however, includes the works of decolonizing reader-writers who adopt various strategies to counteract the violence of imperialism (Harlow: 1–75; Said: 191–262). The following exposition, however, only illustrates some of the literary constructions in colonizing texts, that is, texts designed to take possession of the minds and lands of those who are different.

To begin with characterizations, the colonized and colonizer are sharply contrasted in colonizing literature. The subjugated are depicted as helpless, evil, inarticulate, backward, disorganized, lazy, exotic, and babies in need of instruction.[9] Such characters are put side by side with those in control, civilized, Christian, teachers, articulate, literate, and cultivated. The contrast serves to validate the domination of the former by the latter.

Geographically, the setting of imperial narratives communicates the same ideology, (Blaut: 69–90; Said: 3–43). Some lands are depicted as empty, unoccupied, and waiting to be discovered. Some lands assume the symbol of light and holiness, while the others represent darkness, disease, and evil. The narratives also construct their readers to accept as normal the fact that someone (usually a white man) owns plantations, mines, or farms in other continents, populated and run by native servants. The geography of these narratives generally exhibits a universal and global outlook that invites expansion and relationships of domination and subjugation between nations.

Traveling is also central to colonial narratives. A few travelers,[10] mainly from the metropolitan centers, enter foreign lands. These travelers are notably authoritative strangers, who are not ignorant or dependent upon their hosts. Their authority is grounded on race, religion, technology, and knowledge. They are marked by their power to see deficiency everywhere and to right this deficiency by teaching or structurally developing the colonized people to depend on them. The subjugated may travel to the lands of their masters, but as powerless strangers, such as exiles, slaves, servants, students, or refugees, who depend on the benevolence of their masters.[11]

---

9 For examples of explicit literary colonizing constructions see Conrad and Kipling.

10 The number of colonizing travelers is crucial for it can determine the type and intensity of colonialism experienced by the colonized. For example, in areas where colonizing travelers flooded a colony such as North America, South Africa, Canada, or Australia it led to settler colonialism, which tended to override the native groups.

11 See Segovia: 57–73 on the position of Hispanic-Americans in metropolitan centers of North America.

It is characteristic of colonizing texts to present an extremely gendered perspective of their subject (Quint: 31–41; Manuier: 70; Williams and Chrisman: 194). The colonized lands are to be "entered," "penetrated," and subjugated. The colonized are symbolized by their indigenous women, who epitomize all backwardness, evil, and helplessness. The colonizer's civilization is symbolized by their women as well, who become the measure of their civilization (Strobel: 1–15). The general picture is that imperialism is a male game with women characters articulating men's power positions in it.

It is also characteristic of colonizing texts to conceal their material interests. Nineteenth- and twentieth-century imperialism, for instance, was a power struggle of Western empires prompted by the need to create markets overseas and to import raw materials for their growing industries, but this factor was neatly wrapped in rhetorical terms such as "the duty to the natives." Imperialism was thus presented as a moral vocation to those in need of help; it hardly acknowledged its economic motivation. The hidden motives enable the subjugated to accept their positions to some extent and the colonizers to remain firmly convinced of their good intentions even in the face of overt violence.

In sum, post-colonial texts are born in settings of intense power struggle and they articulate that struggle. In particular, colonizing texts propound relationships of profound inequality, they are driven by expansionist aims, they exhibit fear of difference, they promote the authority of certain traveling strangers, and they have the tendency to disguise their economic interests under moral claims. As Jerry Phillips defines it:

> Imperialism—a system of economic, political, and cultural force that disavows borders in order to extract desirable resources and exploit an alien people—has never stayed away from a field of pedagogical imperatives, what might be called an ideology of instruction. Christianity, Progress, Democracy, or whatever is the prevailing imperialist version of history demands certain cultures, nations, or chosen races that they subject those who fall radically short of the ideal state. Subject people are "savage," "infantile," "untutored," "backward," or simply "underdeveloped"; as the imperialist encounters them, a model of their "uplift" is always thus entailed. (26)

Given the global impact of imperialism and its persistence, post-colonial theorists argue that its models of relationships are among the many bedrocks of oppression in most canonized texts of literature. They point out that bracketing of imperialism as a category in Western academic schools serves to maintain the potency of these oppressive images in our thinking as well as to justify the subjugation of some nations and lands by the imperialistic metropolitan centers (Achebe: 1–20; Said: 41–43, 60–61). For this reason, I turn to arguing for the integration of post-colonial analysis into the liberationist vision of feminist biblical readers.

INTERSECTING FEMINISM AND POST-COLONIALISM IN OUR PRACTICE

With regard to white Western feminism and post-colonialism, it has been noted that the former often brackets imperialism in its analysis of male texts, or operates within imperialist frameworks of power (Lorde: 66–71; Mohanty: 51–80). In her book *Decolonizing Feminisms*, Laura Donaldson highlights that feminist readers use "anti-sexist rhetoric to displace questions of colonialism, racism, and their concomitant violence" (62). Donaldson points out that some feminists have theorized that man=colonizer and woman's body=colonized, a metaphorical articulation which, she notes, can be theoretically defended, but one which often fails to address colonialism as a form of oppression (4–6). The latter position often obscures the fact that Western women were and are equally involved in and benefit from the imperialist oppression of Two-Thirds World women, a position that is still economically and politically in place.

The question for feminist biblical practitioners, therefore, is how to integrate post-colonial insights to their liberation discourse. Given the imperialist setting of the New Testament literature, I would propose that it is imperative for feminist inclusive readings to be more suspicious of imperialism legitimation. If, for example, Matthew characterizes Pilate's wife as a prophetic woman in the trial of Jesus, an inclusive reading must be wary that this positive construction may not necessarily articulate a liberative inclusion of an outsider woman; rather, it may serve to legitimate the imperialist presence by presenting it as holy and acceptable. Elaine Wainwright's feminist inclusive reading of Matthew, for example, demonstrates insufficient suspicion toward the implied author's motivations in constructing Pilate's wife as a divine agent (285–86).

Paying attention to the imperialist setting of the New Testament will also necessitate a more careful assessment of inclusive versus exclusive traditions. In this setting of a struggle for power and survival against imperial forces, an "inclusive" impulse may signal an imperialist collaboration, while an "exclusive" approach may signal a strategic resistance of imperialist powers. For instance, interpretations of Matt 10:5–6, 15:24, and 28:18–20 must weigh out these alternatives within a Roman setting of imperialist occupation and resistance. When post-colonial analysis is integrated, the celebration of "Christian inclusiveness" versus "Jewish exclusiveness" in an imperial setting may have to be re-evaluated.[12] A post-colonial analysis necessitates identifying the Roman Empire as the enemy and the Jewish emphasis on cultural bound-

---

12 I am aware that rigid nationalism is oppressive even to its own people, but more especially to women. Nonetheless, nationalistic movements of the colonized must be seen within their contexts as a strategy of resisting the bigger enemy and as a temporary phase. Indeed, many colonized nations of the modern era adopted and used this strategy effectively.

aries as one of strategic resistance in the face of imposed political leadership, religion, images, languages, and taxes (Horsley: 1–116). This framework immediately calls into question the vision of Matt 28:18–20. That is, if the Jewish people of Matthew's time were struggling to maintain their cultural boundaries against the intrusion of the Roman Empire, does not Matthew's opening of boundaries, his agenda of discipling the whole world according to the commands of Christ, indicate a collaborative stance? Matthew's command to christianize the world ironically befriends the Roman Empire's political and cultural imposition of its structures on Jewish people and all its colonized subjects. It is when we remind ourselves that first-century Palestinian Jews were struggling to survive against the Roman Empire that Matthew's universal commission becomes a suspicious agenda—one which is driven by competition with other local groups for power and one which is consistent with the imperial ideology of disavowing boundaries and claiming cultural authority over foreign people and lands then resisting imperialism. In turn, the questioning of Matthew's worldwide agenda also helps us to understand why Christian missions (read reader-believer-actor of the Christian texts) have functioned compatibly with imperialist agendas of their countries. It also calls for a post-colonial feminist reimagining of Christian mission texts.

Similarly, the gendered construction of imperialist narratives is evident in the featuring of female characters of questionable morality and status in stories representing the penetration of other lands. A good example is Rahab, the prostitute, who becomes the point of contact in the possession of Jericho. Likewise, in both John and Matthew the Samaritan and Canaanite woman are featured in stories foreshadowing the universal mission, that is, the penetration of other lands. Both these women are characterized as either helpless or immoral, symbolizing the status of their own people and thus authorizing the subjugation of their lands. Although these women are celebrated by feminists, a post-colonial analysis detects an ideology of subjugation that proceeds by negative labelling and the use of female gender to articulate relations of subordination and domination.

A post-colonial analysis also indicates that gender experiences in imperialist settings are different, depending on one's relation to the imperialist powers. Among the subjugated groups, women are burdened by two patriarchal systems, the national and the metropolitan one. As the national patriarchal system resists the intrusion of a foreign power, the call for protection of tradition intensifies gender constructions (Harlow: 28–30; Petersen: 251–54). The enemy is the outsider and resistance calls women and men to remain faithful to national traditions. In intertestamental times, both Essenes and Pharisees are representative of this type of resistance. However, the opposite response is also common. In various revolutions and in struggles against imperialism, gender roles are often relaxed for some time, until the groups are established. Thereafter women are put back to their original places. The Jesus movement and the early church represents this type of resistance.

While women on the side of the imperialist automatically belong to a higher class, race, and sometimes religion, they still remain male objects. As attested by the biblical examples of Herod's and Pilate's wives, they are subject to male constructions in the maintenance of male power. Nonetheless, the issues of class, race, and religion are still factors of difference, among the colonized and the colonizer women. Thus a feminist inclusive reading cannot equate the experience of Pilate's wife with that of the mother of Andrew, the son of Zebedee, without taking into account the former's imperialist status of exploiter and oppressor.

This brings me to a crucial question: Which feminist should read from a post-colonial perspective? As the above comments indicate, imperialism has affected all of us and its narratives construct both the powerful and the powerless—all of those who pass through formal education are inducted to accept their positions. Therefore, imperialism involves both Western and Two-Thirds World women, women of color and white women, developed and the so-called underdeveloped countries, precisely because imperialism was and still is a global event and conception that has left little or no place untouched; hence, it informs our perception of the Other.

No doubt Two-Thirds World women suffer more from imperialist intrusion; hence, they are more conscious of it. Western feminist readers, on the other hand, benefit from their social location. They can, consciously or unconsciously, bracket out a post-colonial analysis. The bracketing, however, does not only speak of one's privileged position; it also plays into the maintenance of imperialist metropolitan centers' constructions, and, worse, it hinders building "political coalitions" of resistance among feminists of various cultural persuasions (Tolbert: 312–14).

READING FOR DECOLONIZATION

Among biblical and theological feminist readers, the challenge to read post-colonially for decolonization, that is, the struggle to counter imperialist violence and to seek liberating ways of interdependence, is often presented by women from Two-Thirds World settings. Kwok Pui-lan, for instance, writes that "Christianity as it existed in the West had a right not only to conquer the world but to define reality for other peoples of the world" (303).[13] Rosemary Edet and Bette Ekeya point out that among African people "there is alienation because evangelization has not been that of cultural exchange but of cultural domination and assimilation" (3). This challenge calls for a feminist reading that does not only recover or reconstruct women's par-

---

13 Kwok quotes Hutchinson: 172.

ticipation in early church history, but also strives to re-envision the Christian mission. For instance, how do passages like Matthew 28:18–20, Luke 24: 46–47 and John 20:21 construct the power relations in the encounter with the Other? Do they propose relationships of liberating interdependence[14] between races, genders, cultures, and nations or do they propose a model of unequal inclusion? Kwok Pui-lan, grappling with the biblical models of international exchange, has suggested a "dialogical model of truth," whereby two different and equal subjects meet, and their word to each other is, "What treasures do you have to share?" (Kwok: 313). Such an invitation does not encounter the Other as a blank slate to be filled.

Therefore, conscious awareness of the fact that biblical texts were born in an imperialist setting and have been unique in sponsoring imperialist agendas over different times and people needs to be integrated in our feminist reading for liberation. This requires recognizing that many women in biblical religions also belong to Native American religions, African religions, and Asian religions; that this position is not only intricately related to imperialism, but must also inform our practice. This recognition implies that we are here as women in biblical religion together *with* our Other canons, written and unwritten, and they demand to be heard and read in their own right. I emphasize "other canons" because imperialism proceeds by denying the validity of the narratives and values of its victims, while it imposes its own "master narratives" on them. Furthermore, most of us experienced the Christian mission not as a liberating egalitarian movement, but as a divinely authorized patriarchal and imperial program that subjugates all those who are not Christian. Consequently, unless feminist liberation readers want to stand in continuum with the imperialist "right" of the West "to define reality for other people," the challenge is with us. It is imperative for the "women-church"[15] to become a post-colonial open-space and to read for decolonization—a practice that recognizes that we are already inscribed within an established tradition of imperial domination, collaboration, and resistance. To read for decolonization, therefore, is to consciously resist the exploitative forces of imperialism, to affirm the denied differences, and to seek liberating ways of interdependence in our multi-cultural and post-colonial world.

In this post-colonial interpretive open-space, feminist decolonizing readings should encourage "solidarity in multiplicity." Donaldson defines

---

14 See Said: 3–43, 303–36.

15 Schüssler Fiorenza (1985:126–27) uses the term "women-church" to describe a feminist hermeneutical center. I am extending the boundaries of this center because for survivors of imperialism the invitation to inhabit the "ekklesia," the white male, most hierarchical and exclusive of centers, dangerously befriends the ideology of imperialism that invites its subjects to yearn for their standards even as it structurally denies them access, while at the same time denying the colonized their difference. The colonized, in other words, can enter the "ekklesia" if they forego their cultures, pursue those of their masters, or agree that their cultural values are inferior.

solidarity in multiplicity as a "story field" that affirms "stories" and "demands that each story negotiate its position in relation to all other stories included within the field, which in turn must recalculate their own position" (139). To translate the approach to feminist academic biblical studies, it calls for a practice of reading, imagining, and retelling biblical stories in negotiation with other religious stories in the post-colonial era. Anything short of this risks maintaining the "right" of the Christian biblical stories to remain at the highest peak of the hierarchy—a hierarchy sustained through the suppression of all other religious stories and the oppression of Two-Thirds World women.

How Can We Know and Respect the Other?[16]

Evidently, the main objective of a decolonizing reading is beyond just providing a deconstructive analysis that exposes the imperialist construction embedded in narratives. A decolonizing reading's main objective is liberation. It asks the question: "How can we know and respect the Other?" It is a struggle to conceive models that are not built along the lines of relegating all differences to deficiency. It is a struggle to build bridges for liberating interdependence cross-culturally. It is the desire to begin what have been termed "difficult dialogues" (Phillips: 40–41),[17] that is, to encounter and to dialogue with the different Other on a level of different and equal subjects.

At this level, a post-colonial feminist who reads for decolonization will ask how the Christian texts construct and legitimate encounter with people of different faith, race, gender, and sexuality. The phrase "difficult dialogues," indeed, accepts the fact that the construction of our narratives, hence, our thinking of the Other, has primarily operated on what Phillips has shown to be a denigrate and "uplift" model. In this imperialist model we have an aggressive inclusion but not equality. Consequently, to engage in cultivating "difficult dialogues," feminist readers must indeed become decolonizing readers: they must demonstrate awareness of imperialism as a persistent and exploitative force at a global scale, they must demonstrate a conscious adoption of resistance to imperialism, and they must struggle to map liberating ways of interdependence in our multi-cultural world. To bracket decolonizing is only to maintain the imperial strategies of exploitation and subjugation and to hinder building the necessary "political coalitions" among feminists of different cultures, nations, colors, classes, and sexuality.

---

16 See Williams: 8. This is Edward Said's central question in his post-colonial work.

17 Phillips (40–41) traces this term to Johnella Butler ("Difficult Dialogues," in *Women's Review of Books* 6: 5 [1989] p. 16) who used it to describe "cultural negotiation between opposing ends of the earth," and Phillips uses it to point out that "for too long we have not listened to what others have to say."

Conclusion

In sum, the Bible as a Western book is bound to its imperialist history of subjugation and oppression. This imperialist history has constructed all of us, and its reality cannot be bracketed from our critical practice without perpetuating the history of unequal inclusion. The biblical story is at times a travel narrative; it commands its readers to travel. Consequently, the privileging of one historical time, the ancient times, in determining its meaning is ideologically suspect. Moreover, women in biblical religion also stand in other religions. The challenge, therefore, is to become decolonizing readers, who seek to build true conversations of equal subjects in our post-colonial and multi-cultural world. Without overlooking the differences of race, sexuality, religion, and class, I am proposing that our critical practice should be multi-cultural in a post-colonial open-space of women of the world as equal subjects.

Works Consulted

Achebe, Chinua
    1989   *Hopes and Impediments: Selected Essays*. New York: Doubleday.

Appiah, Kwame Anthony
    1992   *In My Father's House: Africa in the Philosophy of Culture*. New York: Oxford University Press.

Ashcroft, Bill, Gareth Griffiths, and Helen Tiffin
    1989   *The Empire Writes Back: Theory and Practice in Post-colonial Literatures*. New York: Routledge.

    1995   *The Post-colonial Studies Reader*. New York: Routledge.

Bach, Alice, ed.
    1990   *The Pleasure of Her Text: Feminist Readings of Biblical and Historical Texts*. Philadelphia: Trinity.

Bhabha, Homi K.
    1995   *The Location of Culture*. London: Routledge.

Blaut, James M.
    1993   *The Colonizer's Model of the World: Geographical Diffusionism and Eurocentric History*. New York: Guilford.

Blunt, Alison
    1994   *Travel, Gender, and Imperialism: Mary Kingsley and West Africa*. New York: Guilford.

Blunt, Alison and Gillian Rose, eds.
    1994   *Writing Women and Space: Colonial and Postcolonial Geographies*. New York: Guilford.

Cannon, Katie
1987   "Slave Ideology and Biblical Interpretation." *Semeia* 47 (1987):9–23.

Conrad, Joseph
1981   *Heart of Darkness, and The Secret Sharer.* Bantam Classic. [1902].

Donaldson, Laura
1992   *Decolonizing Feminisms: Race, Gender, and Empire-building.* Chapel Hill:
          University of North Carolina Press.

Edet, Rosemary and Bette Ekeya
1988   "Church Women of Africa: A Theological Community." Pp. 3–13 in *With
          Passion and Compassion. Third World Women Doing Theology: Reflections
          from the Women's Commission of the EATWT.* Ed. Virginia Fabella and
          Mercy Amba Oduyoye. Maryknoll, NY: Orbis.

Fewell, Danna Nolan and David M. Gunn
1993   *Gender, Power, & Promise: The Subject of the Bible's First Story.* Nashville:
          Abingdon.

Harlow, Barbara
1987   *Resistance Literature.* New York: Methuen.

Horsley, Richard A.
1993   *Jesus and the Spiral of Violence: Popular Jewish Resistance in Roman Palestine.*
          Minneapolis: Fortress.

Hutchinson, W. R.
1982   "A Moral Equivalent for Imperialism: Americans and the Promotion of
          Christian Civilization, 1880–1910." In *Missionary Ideologies in the Imperi-
          alist Era: 1880–1920.* Ed. T. Christensen and W. R. Hutchinson. Aarhus:
          Aros.

Kipling, Rudyard
1962   "The White Man's Burden." Pp. 87–88 in *The Imperialism Reader.* Ed.
          Louis Snyder. New York: Van Nostrand.

Kwok, Pui-lan
1991   "Discovering the Bible in the Non-biblical World." Pp. 299–315 in *Voices
          from the Margin. Interpreting the Bible in the Third World.* Ed. R. S. Su-
          girtharajah. Maryknoll, NY: Orbis.

Lind, Christopher
1995   *Something's Wrong Somewhere: Globalization, Community and the Moral
          Economy of the Farm Crisis.* Halifax: Fernwood.

Lorde, Audre
1984   *Sister Outsider: Essays and Speeches.* Calfornia: Crossing.

Luz, Ulrich
1994   *Matthew in History: Interpretation, Influence, and Effects.* Minneapolis:
          Fortress.

Martyn, J. Louis
    1979   *History and Theology in the Fourth Gospel*. Nashville: Abingdon.

Maunier, Rene
    1949   *The Sociology of Colonies: An Introduction to the Study of Colonies*. Vol. 1. London: Routledge.

Mazrui, Ali A.
    1990   *Cultural Forces in World Politics*. London: James Curry.

    1994   *The Idea of Africa*. Bloomington: Indiana University Press.

Meeks, Wayne
    1983   *The First Urban Christians: The Social World of the Apostle Paul*. New Haven: Yale University Press.

Mohanty, Chandra
    1991   "Under Western Eyes: Feminist Scholarship and Colonial Discourses." Pp. 51–80 in *Third World Women and the Politics of Feminism*. Ed. Chandra Mohanty, Ann Russo, and Lourdes Torres. Bloomington: Indiana University Press.

Morrison, Toni
    1990   *Playing in the Dark: Whiteness and Literary Imagination*. New York: Vintage.

Mudimbe, V. Y.
    1988   *The Invention of Africa: Gnosis, Philosophy and the Order of Knowledge*. Bloomington: Indiana University Press.

Phillips, Jerry
    1993   "Educating the Savages: Melville, Bloom, and the Rhetoric of Imperialist Tradition." Pp. 25–44 in *Recasting the World: Writing after Colonialism*. Ed. Jonathan White. Baltimore: The Johns Hopkins University Press.

Pratt, Mary Louise
    1992   *Imperial Eyes: Travel Writing and Transculturation*. New York: Routledge.

Quint, David
    1993   *Epic and Empire*. Princeton: Princeton University Press.

Said, Edward
    1993   *Culture and Imperialism*. New York: Alfred A. Knopf.

Schüssler Fiorenza, Elisabeth
    1985   "The Will to Choose or to Reject: Continuing Our Critical Work." Pp. 125–36 in *Feminist Interpretation of the Bible*. Ed. Letty Russell. Philadelphia: Westminster.

    1992   *But She Said: Feminist Practices of Biblical Interpretation*. Boston: Beacon.

Segovia, Fernando F.
    1995   "Toward a Hermeneutics of the Diaspora: A Hermeneutics of Otherness and Engagement." Pp. 57–73 in *Reading from This Place. Volume 1: Social*

Location and Biblical Interpretation in the United States. Ed. Fernando F. Segovia and Mary Ann Tolbert. Minneapolis: Fortress.

Strobel, Margaret
1991   *European Women and the Second British Empire*. Bloomington: Indiana University Press.

Tolbert, Mary Ann
1990   "Protestant Feminists and the Bible: On the Horns of a Dilemma." Pp. 5–23 in *The Pleasure of Her Text: Feminist Readings of Biblical and Historical Texts*. Ed. Alice Bach. Philadelphia: Trinity.

1995   "Politics and Poetics of Location." Pp. 305–17 in *Reading From This Place. Volume 1: Social Location and Biblical Interpretation in the United States*. Ed. Fernando F. Segovia and Mary Ann Tolbert. Minneapolis: Fortress.

Wainwright, Elaine
1991   *Towards a Feminist Critical Reading of the Gospel according to Matthew*. Berlin: de Gruyter.

White, Jonathan, ed.
1993   *Recasting the World: Writing after Colonialism*. Baltimore: The Johns Hopkins University Press.

Wicker O'Brien, Kathleen
1993   "Teaching Feminist Biblical Studies in a Postcolonial Context." Pp. 367–80 in *Searching the Scriptures: A Feminist Introduction*. Ed. Elisabeth Schüssler Fiorenza. New York: Crossroad.

Williams, Patrick and Laura Chrisman, eds.
1994   *Colonial Discourse and Post-colonial Theory: A Reader*. New York: Columbia University Press.

CHILDLESSNESS AND WOMAN-TO-WOMAN RELATIONSHIPS IN GENESIS AND IN AFRICAN PATRIARCAL SOCIETY: SARAH AND HAGAR FROM A ZIMBABWEAN WOMAN'S PERSPECTIVE (GEN 16:1–16; 21:8–21)

Dora R. Mbuwayesango
Hood Theological Seminary

ABSTRACT

The article looks at the Sarah and Hagar narratives (Gen 16:1–16; 21:8–21) in the context of Ndebele and Shona patriarchal societies of Zimbabwe. The role of women in the narratives and in Ndebele and Shona societies is similar, that is, child-bearing. The view of barrenness is almost similar, except that in the Genesis narratives the concept of male sterility does not seem to be a consideration. In both cases the women have to provide the solution to barrenness. In the Genesis narratives, Sarah is presented without any help from her kin, while in the Ndebele and Shona societies, the problem of a woman's barrenness is solved by her kin group and not by her alone. Inheritance is a major issue in the Genesis narratives and in the Ndebele and Shona societies.

In the book of Genesis, the interaction between women is depicted in the context of narratives dealing with the problem of childlessness. There are two cases that portray female relationships. One is between Sarah and Hagar (Gen 16:1–16; 21:8–21).[1] The other is between two sisters, Rachel and Leah, married to the same man, Jacob (Gen 30:1–24). One of the women in each case is able to have children while the other is not. This article seeks to look at the relationship between Sarai and Hagar from an African patriarchal society's perspective, particularly from that of the Ndebele and Shona peoples of Zimbabwe.

WOMEN AND CHILDLESSNESS IN NDEBELE AND SHONA SOCIETIES

The most important role of women in African patriarchal society is that of child-bearing. In the Ndebele and Shona societies, this is reflected in the marriage system. Marriage is characterized by what is called the *lobola* system in which a man transfers some designated property, usually cattle, to his

---

1 The names of Sarai and Abram change in chapter 21 to Sarah and Abraham respectively.

wife's family. An exact interpretation of the function of *lobola* is "child-price" because this is payment that is intended to support a patrilineal system of descent. The male pays to ensure paternal immortality through his children, particularly sons.

Lobola demonstrates in two different ways the importance of women's ability to bear children in the Ndebele and Shona societies. In the Ndebele marriage system *lobola* is only paid when the woman is already pregnant. In the Shona society, the process of the payment is usually started before children are born. In both societies there is a strong understanding that a man by merely making a woman pregnant does not thereby become entitled to the child. The child becomes his only when he has given *lobola* to his in-laws to transfer the status of the child as a member of the maternal group to that of the paternal group.[2]

The importance of child-bearing is further demonstrated in the Shona society by the practice of *kugadza mapfihwa* in which a married woman is only given her own cooking place (Shona: *mapfihwa*) after bearing her first child. Prior to that she is regarded and treated as a child and her mother-in-law is her overseer. The giving of a cooking place to a woman is accompanied by celebration where she cooks the first meal in her own cooking place. A woman childless is regarded as a child who is told what to cook by her mother or mother-in-law. To be considered a mature woman, a woman has to have the right to select daily meals. This is one of the rites of passage in women's development process from childhood to womanhood in the Shona society. Although in Ndebele society a homestead is given to a man at marriage, the status of women is almost contingent on motherhood, just as in the Shona society. One is not considered a mature woman until one's male kin have received *lobola*, which can only be paid when the woman is pregnant. This means that for a woman to have a significant status in society she must bear a child.

If a sexual union does not result in pregnancy at the expected time, arrangements are made so that the wife has sexual intercourse with one of her husband's brothers.[3] If after having sexual relations with her husband's brother, she does not conceive, then it is concluded that she is to blame. It is important to realize that this is simultaneously a test as well as a solution. The problem of barrenness or premature death of a married woman is remedied through the practice of *bondwe* or *chimutsamapfihwa* in Shona and *um-thanyelo* or *imbokokodo* in Ndebele. Through these practices a supplement is provided to fill up the gap created by the lack of children. Prior to the colonial era, the problem was dealt with before it even occurred. When a woman was

---

2 The concept of illegitimate children is foreign to Shona and Ndebele societies.

3 The Shona and Ndebele concept of brother includes one's cousins but in this case it is limited to paternal cousins or male members of the kin group.

married she was given a girl, usually a sister or niece (classificatory sister), to accompany her, with the understanding that if any misfortune such as barrenness or premature death should occur, this young woman would stand in for her.[4] In most cases the girl was very young so that her elder sister or aunt had the responsibility of raising her and eventually helping her find a good husband.

The status of women in Ndebele and Shona societies is also reflected in the area of inheritance. Females do not occupy a hereditary position in their patrilineage or that of their husbands. In both cultures, the eldest son is the primary inheritor or successor of a deceased man.[5] It is birth date that determines who is to be the primary inheritor. Thus the son of a junior wife can be the primary inheritor. But it is important to realize that this is not just settled by birth date; in most cases it is settled on who was the strongest. There are many stories in Ndebele and Shona folklore that depict inheritance disputes, especially in royal families.

Since African marriage was characterized by polygamy, inheritance disputes were very common. In order to avoid bloody disputes, a man was generally encouraged to marry women from the same kin group. This was an attempt to avoid the problems that occurred in polygamy, especially when the wives were not related. If the wives were from the same kin group, then disputes among them were decided by representatives from their kin group, i.e. paternal aunts and uncles.

The value of women in Ndebele and Shona societies is still determined by their biological reproductive capability, although, in most cases, the practice of providing a supplement is no longer applied. Usually, the husband prefers to get another wife independently, and it is left to the childless woman to stay or to leave the man. If a man does not take any measures to find a way of having children, it is generally concluded that the problem is with the man. Nevertheless, it is women who are penalized for being infertile and not men.

Women and Childlessness in Gen 16:1–16; 21:8–12

Sarai is one of the two women introduced in the outline of the descendants of Terah, the father of Abraham (Gen 11:27–30). She is introduced as the wife of Abram, Terah's son. It is striking that while the genealogy is being given from a male perspective, it is Sarai and not Abram who is said to be "barren" and that "she had no child" (Gen 11:30). It becomes evident that Sarai is depicted as responsible for Abram's lack of children. In Genesis 16:1

---

4 Any woman from the kin group can act as a stand-in or representation of another woman from the same kin group, just as any man can do the same for another male of his kin group.

5 For more details on the issue of inheritance see May; Folbre: 61–80; Mair: 9–20.

it is stated that "Sarai did not bear children for Abram." Unlike the case of Jacob where one of his wives, namely Leah, had children (Gen 30), Abram is not reported as having any other wife who had borne him children. The narrator does not tell us how it was determined that Sarai, not Abram nor even both of them, was responsible for their childlessness.

Sarai is presented as having a problem, failing to provide children for Abram, but she is also presented as having a solution. It is said, "Sarai did not bear children for Abram but she had a שפחה מצרית ('an Egyptian *shiphah*') whose name was Hagar" (Gen 16:1). The story starts with a negative note, the problem of barrenness, which is immediately followed by a positive note introduced by "but."[6] It seems the social status of a woman in the Hebrew Bible in general depends on the woman's ability or inability to have children (Bird: 41–88). Sarai is presented as having a way to influence how she would be positioned in the patriarchal society. Another woman would bear a child on Sarai's behalf to remove the stigma of childlessness. Yahweh had closed her womb but she was determined to overcome this barrier (Gen 16:2a). Therefore, she allows Abram to have sex with Hagar so that she "may be built up through her" (Gen 16:2b).

The meaning of the term שפחה is not clear in the English language. It is usually taken to be synonymous with אמה, which is translated "female slave" or "female servant." But it is important to note that the functions of the two are never depicted as interchangeable. In the book of Genesis, the woman who is given by a wife to her husband for the purpose of bearing children is always a שפחה, never אמה. If אמה is a female slave or servant, then שפחה is something else, but different from a slave or a servant. The term seems to indicate a woman by whom a man could legitimately have children apart from his first wife (Gen 12:16) or through whom another woman could have children (Gen 30:1–24).

The term used to refer to what Hagar becomes to Abram is אשה ("woman, wife"). Some scholars interpret this to mean that Hagar becomes Abram's concubine or harlot (Waters: 190; Speiser: 116–17; Vawter: 213–14). But Sarai gives Hagar to Abram to be his wife (Gen 16:3), for the term אשה simply means woman or wife. Thus Sarai does not give Hagar to Abram to be his concubine or harlot but wife.

Initially, the arrangement of Hagar, Sarai, and Abram seems to be working because when Abram has sexual relations with Hagar she conceives. But something happens to upset this arrangement. What really happened is not clear but it is depicted in terms of Sarai's status in the eyes of Hagar. The narrator tells us that something happened to Hagar's view of Sarai—Sarai "became small in her eyes" (Gen 16:4). What Hagar does is not clear, but also

---

6 See Lambdin: 162–63 on disjunctive clauses.

Sarai does not confront Hagar. It seems that the consequences of Hagar's realization that she had conceived are presented as though they were not within her control. This explains why Sarai did not confront her but instead goes to Abram who was obliged to help in correcting Hagar's perspective of Sarai. Whatever is wrong in the relationship between Sarai and Hagar, Abram has the key to make it right. In some sense, it seems, Abram is the cause of this rift between the two women. In fact Sarai says her grievance is with Abram (Gen 16:5a).

Abram shifts the responsibility to Sarai by pointing out that Hagar was Sarai's responsibility. Sarai gave Hagar to Abram to be his wife but he wants Hagar to be treated as Sarai's שפחה. Abram declares, "Your שפחה is in your hand, do to her what is good in your eyes" (Gen 16:6). It appears Abram is rejecting Hagar as his wife.

Since most scholars consider Hagar to be Sarai's slave, it is readily interpreted that Sarai made Hagar do difficult tasks. But this interpretation seems to be based on preconceived ideas. The word ענה is the same as the one used in the book of Exodus to indicate what the "sons of Israel" went through in Egypt (Exod 1:1–22).[7] It seems that here the Egyptian king was concerned about the population growth of the Israelites. He is concerned that the Israelites are going to become numerous and in case of war they might join Egypt's enemies. Therefore, he is interested in thwarting the population growth of the Israelites by dealing with them harshly. The method used in the book of Exodus to thwart or frustrate the Israelites is hard labor. In the case of Hagar, the method Sarai uses to frustrate her is not described.

Hagar's response to Sarai's attempts to frustrate her is to flee (Gen 16:6). Hagar's flight is taken by some interpreters to be a sign that she was indignantly refusing to be oppressed by Sarai. According to Trible, "episode one closes with Hagar taking command of her own life . . ." (13). But it is more a sign of hopelessness and helplessness. She does not know to whom to turn so she takes refuge in the wilderness.

The messenger of Yahweh finds Hagar in the wilderness at a well on the way to Shur (Gen 16:7). Shur is identified as southwest of Palestine on the eastern border of Egypt (Baly and Tushingham: 104). The messenger of Yahweh identifies Hagar as Sarai's שפחה and asks her where she is coming from and where she is going (Gen 16:8). Here is an indication that Hagar is still identified in relationship to Sarai. And Hagar says she is running away from Sarai, which could mean that Hagar is also seeing herself in relationship to Sarai (Gen 16:9). Hagar does not respond to the second part of the question, which means she does not know where she is going. If Hagar is viewed as an oppressed slave of Sarai, then the advice of the messenger to

---

[7] The range of meanings of the Assyrian cognate *enû* includes "thwart" and "frustrate" (Brown, Driver, and Briggs: 776).

Hagar is surprising—for Hagar to go back to Sarai (Gen 16:9). What Hagar is to do when she goes back, to "restrain herself," is a verb in the hithpolel (הִתְעַנִּי) from the same root as what Sarai does to her which was in piel (תְּעַנֶּה). According to Trible (16), Hagar is told to go back to oppression and suffering. But it seems this had to do with the restoration of Sarai and Hagar's relationship to the state it was before she became Abram's wife, i.e. Hagar as Sarah's שִׁפְחָה. It is important to realize that she is being told to go back to Sarai, and not to Abram, her husband. Abram's action or rather lack of action as far as Hagar's status is concerned indicates that Hagar has no future with Abram.

The messenger promises Hagar that she was going to be an important person outside the constrains of patriarchy—her offspring would be multiplied not as Abram's offspring. The promise is made to Hagar directly (Gen 16:10).

The narrative concludes with a description of the birth of Hagar's son. Sarai does not seem to play a part in the process of the birth of Ishmael (Gen 16:15–16). This is different from the account of Leah and Rachel because these latter two are depicted as naming the children who are borne for them (Gen 30:6, 8, 11, 13). The narrative concludes without showing us whether or not the relationship between Sarai and Hagar is restored.

When we next see Sarah and Hagar in relationship to each other (Gen 21: 8–21), the circumstances differ. Many scholars take these narratives to be another version of the same story in Genesis 16 (J) from the E source (e.g. Skinner: 285). In addition, however, these narratives in their present location are meant to depict different scenes in the patriarchal narratives (Trible: 9; Teubal: 22). Both women now have sons. The context of the narrative is the celebration of the weaning of Isaac, Sarah's son (Gen 21:8). Sarah sees Hagar's son, who is not named in this narrative (Gen 21:9), but we know that it is Ishmael, whom Hagar is said to have borne for Abraham (Gen 16:15–16). What he is doing is expressed plainly, but the exact meaning has always been a subject of speculation. After the word מְצַחֵק, "playing", "with Isaac" is often added on the basis of the LXX and the Vulgate. Some suggest it implies that Ishmael was mocking Isaac. According to Hertz, מְצַחֵק refers to an act of impurity and idolatry and he translates verse 9 as "Ishmael laughed derisively at the feasting and rejoicing" (176). Others go as far as suggesting that Ishmael was abusing Isaac.[8] But this seems to be an attempt to justify Sarah's harshness; as Speiser rightly points out, "מצחק without a preposition cannot mean "to mock" (155). It seems the sentence as a whole is describing how Hagar's son fits into the picture—"Sarah saw the son of Hagar, whom she had borne for Abraham, playing." Thus Abraham now has two sons and the

---

8 See examples in Vawter: 248–49; cf. Gal 4:21–31.

relationship of the two women is now governed by the place of the two sons
in relationship to Abraham.

The issue concerns inheritance. The subject of inheritance is one of the
major themes in the book of Genesis. There are stories that attempt to explain
why the eldest son is not the primary inheritor, the narratives about Esau
and Jacob (Gen 25:19–27:40). Thus Hagar's son is Abraham's elder son and
therefore the primary inheritor. The problem is indicated by Sarah's refusal to present the two sons as Abraham's sons. She refers to Isaac as "my
son" and to Ishmael as "the son of the servant." Sarah is concerned with
Abraham's relationship to Hagar's son and not with Hagar's relationship to
Abraham. It is not simply jealousy that moves Sarah to demand the expulsion of Hagar and her son.

At the sight of Hagar's son, Sarah says to Abraham, "Cast out this female
servant (slave) and her son; indeed the son of this servant will not inherit with
my son, Isaac" (Gen 21:10). In chapter 16 Sarai referred to Hagar as her שפחה
but now she refers to her as אמה. (It is also possible that originally, it was
simply אשה but was changed in transmission to reflect the hatred between the
Israelites and Ishmaelites.) She uses a highly derogatory term to refer to
Hagar and what is significant is that she does not refer to Hagar and her son
by their names. It seems Sarah's motive is based primarily on establishing and
securing her son's future. Two sons equally vying for the same status is po-
tentially dangerous (cf. Esau and Jacob). If Hagar had borne a female instead,
she and her child would not have been expelled, since daughters could only
be considered as inheritors if a man did not have sons (Num 27:8).

Abraham is portrayed as being reluctant to do what Sarah says and only
expels Hagar and her sons when the deity, Elohim, sanctions it. Elohim
tells him to listen to Sarah (Gen 21:11–12). It seems Abraham did not know
through which son his lineage was to be. So Elohim assures him that it is
through Isaac and therefore Abraham could expel Hagar's son. Although
Elohim explains that Hagar's son is also going to be made into a nation, the
expulsion of Hagar and her son seem very unfair. We are again presented
with a woman in a desperate situation who has fulfilled the most important requirement of patriarchy for a woman, child-bearing, but is rejected
by patriarchy (Gen 21:14). Hagar is once more in the wilderness, now with
no water and a son about to starve to death, when Elohim appears to her
(Gen 21:15–19). Significantly Elohim does not instruct her to go back either to
Sarah or to Abraham, nor even to Egypt. Hagar and her son dwell in the
wilderness (Gen 21:21).

CONCLUSION: GEN 16:1–16; 21:8–21 IN THE NDEBELE AND SHONA CONTEXT

The role of Sarah in the book of Genesis parallels the role of women
in Ndebele and Shona societies, namely child-bearing. But there are some

significant differences. The connection of Sarah to her kin is not depicted. In fact, she uses an Egyptian woman who is best understood as her companion. Thus when problems arise between her and Hagar, there is no one to intervene. But in Ndebele and Shona societies the woman's kin play a major role in providing the supplement and in supervising the relationship of the women.

I would like to point out briefly some of the disturbing aspects of the Sarah and Hagar narratives. One aspect is the apparent endorsement of the patriarchal value system in regard to the status of women in society. The fact that the second narrative concludes with Sarah having a son serves to reinforce the idea that every woman must fulfill the obligation of bearing children, especially a son. Also, the narratives seem to reject the practice of having one woman stand for another in cases of barrenness. It seems Ishmael does not qualify as Abraham's heir. The narratives, however, fail to provide an alternative. A barren Ndebele or Shona woman would prefer to have an alternative rather than to have no hope at all. But the most ideal position would be to change the value system of the Ndebele and Shona culture. Child-bearing, which, for the most part, is not within a woman's control, should not be used to define a woman's value and status in society.

Like Sarah and Hagar the women in the Shona and Ndebele societies are in a patriarchal web that is not easy to untangle. Although women are victims of patriarchy, they play a very significant part in the empowering and perpetuation of patriarchy. The interaction between Sarah and Hagar is determined by the patriarchal value system. Sarah and Hagar relate to each other in a patriarchal context. Sarah sees Hagar in terms of how she can help her meet her patriarchal obligation—providing children for Abraham. Hagar also sees Sarah and herself through the patriarchal value system. When she sees that she is pregnant, her perspective of Sarah is altered. In the Shona and Ndebele cultures, women's relationships are governed or directed by what society expects from women. Mothers and aunts have the responsibility of making sure that female children fulfill their patriarchal obligation. Their status in society is also determined by how women under their responsibility fare according to the patriarchal expectation.

The role of Yahweh or Elohim in the Genesis narratives is disturbing. In the first narrative, Yahweh is presented endorsing patriarchy. Yahweh tells Hagar to go back to Sarah where she is not happy or comfortable. In the second narrative, Elohim endorses the banishment of Hagar and her son. The role that Yahweh and Elohim play in the Sarah and Hagar stories is played by tradition in the Ndebele and Shona societies. This is what is often referred to as *tsika dzemateteguru* in Shona (customs of the ancestors), which have been a major endorsement of the oppression of women in Zimbabwe.

WORKS CONSULTED

Baly, Denis and A. D. Tushingham
1971   *Atlas of the Biblical World.* New York: World.

Bird, Phyllis
1974   "Images of Women in the Old Testament." Pp. 41–88 in *Religion and Sexism: Images of Women in the Jewish and Christian Traditions.* Ed. Rosemary Radford Ruether. New York: Simon & Schuster.

Brown, Francis, S. R. Driver, and Charles A. Briggs
1907   *Hebrew Lexicon of the Old Testament.* Oxford: Clarendon.

Bullwinckle, Davis A.
1982–83 "Women and their Role in African Society: The Literature of the 70s." *African Affairs* 115:263–91.

Gelfand, Michael
1973   *The Genuine Shona: Survival Values of an African Culture.* Gweru: Mambo.

Hertz, Joseph H.
1929   *Genesis: Pentateuch and Haftorahs with Commentary.* London: Oxford University Press.

Holleman, J. F.
1952   *Shona Customary Law: With Reference to Kinship, Marriage, Family and the Estate.* Manchester: Manchester University Press.

Kanyongo-Male, Diane and Philistia Onyango
1984   *The Sociology of the African Family.* London and New York: Longman.

Lambdin, Thomas O.
1971   *Introduction to Biblical Hebrew.* New York: Scribner's.

Mair, Lucy
1969   *African Marriage and Social Change.* London: Frank Cass.

May, Joan
1987   *Changing People, Changing Laws.* Gweru: Mambo.

Skinner, John
1964   *A Critical and Exegetical Commentary on Genesis.* Edinburgh: T. & T. Clark.

Speiser, E. A.
1964   *Genesis: Introduction, Translation and Notes.* AB 1. Garden City, NY: Doubleday.

Tamez, Elsa
1987   "The Woman who Complicated the History of Salvation." Pp. 5–17 in *New Eyes for Reading: Biblical and Theological Reflections by Women from the Third World.* Ed. John S. Pobee and Barbel von Wartenberg-Potter. Bloomington, IN: Meyer Stone.

Teubal, Savina
  1990   *Hagar the Egyptian: The Lost Tradition of the Matriarchs.* San Francisco:
            Harper & Row.

Trible, Phyllis
  1984   *Texts of Terror: Literary-Feminist Readings of Biblical Narratives.* Philadel-
            phia: Fortress.

Vawter, Bruce
  1977   *On Genesis: A New Reading.* Garden City, NY: Doubleday.

Waters, John W.
  1991   "Who is Hagar?" Pp. 187–205 in *Stony the Road We Trod: African-
            American Biblical Interpretation.* Ed. Cain Hope Felder. Minneapolis:
            Fortress.

Weinrich, A. K. H.
  1982   *African Marriage in Zimbabwe and the Impact of Christianity.* Gweru:
            Mambo.

Weems, Renita J.
  1988   "A Mistress, a Maid, and No Mercy (Hagar and Sarah)." Pp. 1–21 in *Just
            a Sister Away: A Womanist Vision of Women's Relationships in the Bible.* San
            Diego: LuraMedia.

Westermann, Claus
  1985   *Genesis 12–36: A Commentary.* Minneapolis: Augsburg.

Zvobgo, Edson
  1983   "Women in Zimbabwe Removing Laws that Oppress Women." *Africa
            Report* 28:45–47.

HAN-LADEN WOMEN: KOREAN "COMFORT WOMEN" AND WOMEN IN JUDGES 19–21

Yani Yoo
Union Theological Seminary

ABSTRACT

This essay intends to demonstrate how the so-called military comfort women issue can be illuminated through the biblical story of women in Judges 19–21 and vice versa. The biblical story invites the reader to witness and denounce the human evil against fellow human beings, especially women. Both "comfort women" and women in Judges 19–21 were victims of extravagant violence. A Korean psychological term, *han* (a sense of unresolved resentment against injustice suffered), can be a helpful hermeneutical clue to connect these groups of women. They were women of *han* whose wounds were so deep that their souls have been wandering between the world beyond and this world without comfort. The essay calls the reader to resolve their *han* and to stop ongoing violence against women around the world.

I. INTRODUCTION

This essay concerns how a reader of the Bible can understand the issue of the so-called military comfort women (*Jongun Wianbu* or *Jungshindae* in Korean), a distorted term for Korean women who were forced to give sexual service to Japanese soldiers during the colonization of Korea by Japan (1910–1945). Approximately 200,000 Korean women, or 80% of the entire Asian "comfort women" population, were conscripted by deceit or abduction. This hard fact was concealed until the early 1990s. The issue was publicized through the efforts of many women and attained special attention at the women's conference of the United Nations in Beijing in 1995. The Beijing conference requested that the Japanese government fully compensate the victims.

The story in Judges 19–21 is the biblical text with which we can best make an analogy with the "comfort women" issue. While "comfort women" have the twentieth-century Asian setting, the biblical women are found in the eleventh-century BCE Canaanite setting. Many hermeneutical questions and suspicions arise. What relationship exists between the women in Judges 19–21 and "comfort women"? Why do we bring a contemporary reality to the Bible which was shaped as a religious canon a long time ago? What would the Bible say about the issue of "comfort women"? We do not intend to give answers to these questions, but to demonstrate how the "comfort women" story can be illuminated through the biblical story and vice versa. We will first deal with the issue of "comfort women" and analyze the biblical story in Judges 19–21. Then we will try to connect the feelings of these victimized women in terms of *han*, a Korean word for wounded heart, as a hermeneutical clue.

II. CONFLUENCE OF "COMFORT WOMEN" AND WOMEN IN JUDGES 19–21

A. Korean "Comfort Women": Historical Overview[1]

According to Prof. Chung-Ok Yun, both Korean women and men had been used as a labor force by Japan since 1910 when Korea became its colony. In the early stage, Korean women went to Osaka, Japan, to work in the factories there. When they arrived they found out that in most cases their duty was to prostitute themselves for Korean men who were laborers. In this way, the women were forced into prostitution for Korean men at first and then to Japanese men later. The Sino-Japanese war in 1937 resulted in the conscription of 1,150,000 Korean men into forced labor and the Nanking rape of the same year caused the draft of 200,000 Korean women into systemized sexual slavery. In August 1944 Japan officially decreed "The Labor Decree of Women *Jungshin*" and justified "The Service Corps of Women Patriots" and "The Service Corps of Women Laborers," which had already existed.

As survivors testify, the women taken were placed in two categories. The first group of women were Labor *Jungshindae* who were not involved in forced sexual service and worked in munitions or textile factories in Taeku and Pusan in Korea, Shizuoka Numazu, and Matsubara Matsuzo in Japan. The second category concerns us. They were the military "comfort women" who were forced into sexual slavery in Teinchin, Manchuria, Peking, and Shanghai in China, La Paul Island, Singapore, the South Pacific Islands, Saipan Island, and in less well-known places.

Most "comfort women" were confined to small rooms about the size of a double bed and were not allowed to leave except for time for the basic needs. They were raped by dozens of soldiers every day of their confinement. If a woman escaped and was captured, she was brutally tortured. One victim still has a scar on her back from the torture of a hot iron.

---

1 The historical overview on "comfort women" relies on *Jungshindae Issue Materials I* and *Jungshindae Issue Materials II* published by Korean Council for the Women Drafted for Sexual Service by Japan.

As of January 1992, 181 witnesses reported to the Korean Council for the Women Drafted for Sexual Service by Japan: 94 Labor *Jungshindae*, 55 military "comfort women," and 32 unclassified. "Unclassified" comprises reports by the families, relatives, and neighbors of those who did not return.

Where, then, are the rest? First, the Japanese military eliminated evidence about military "comfort women" by shooting, burying alive, and abandoning these women in order to conceal what Japan did to them. Second, it is reported that many "comfort women" committed suicide. Some men witnesses who were returning from the draft in the same ship saw "comfort women" throw themselves into the sea even as the ship neared Korea. Third, some women who could not return settled in foreign countries. Fourth, it is assumed that there must be many among survivors who remain unidentified. We need to point out that Korean patriarchal culture prompted the survivors to commit suicide, discouraged them from coming back to their home country, and made them remain silent over fifty years.

B. Women in Judges 19–21

The biblical story has been studied from many angles. Among others, Stuart Lasine's suggestion interests us: the narrative here intends to reveal the "ludicrous and topsy-turvy nature of the world" (37). But my thesis goes further: through the descriptions of an unnamed woman's gruesome death and the massacre of other women, the story invites the reader to witness and denounce the human evil against fellow human beings, especially women. Through a close reading of the narrative we will pursue this thesis.

Two scenes of hospitality are at work in chapter 19: the Levite's father-in-law's hospitality to the Levite at Bethlehem in Judah and then an old man's hospitality in Gibeah. In the first scene, three main characters are called the Levite/his son-in-law, his concubine[2]/young woman, and his father-in-law/her father or the young woman's father, respectively. Though at a glance these relational terms appear randomly, they are deliberately used to divide the characters into two parties: (1) the Levite and (2) his father-in-law and the woman. The "woman's father" is twice (19:4, 9) in apposition with "his father-in-law," emphasizing the existence of two invisible parties. The frequent occurrences of "her father's house" and "the young woman's father" indicate intimacy between the woman and her father. The Levite is isolated and weakened in the following ways and thus makes a weaker party.

---

2 Mieke Bal insists that the term, *pilegesh*, should be translated as "wife" instead of its common translation, "concubine" (83–86). But we will use the term concubine because it is more fitting than 'wife' to the narrative mood and intention.

First, the man does not belong to the place where he lodges now. The place is called *"her* father's house" (19:2, 3), not *"his* father-in-law's house." Second, the man is totally voiceless, in contrast to his talkative father-in-law. Third, he is controlled by the host, his father-in-law (Jones-Warsaw: 175, n. 2; Yee: 164). The host successfully makes him stay longer. Fourth, the Levite gets even with his concubine. During his stay at "her father's house," the narrator never calls him "the Levite" which indicates a higher social status, nor the woman *"his concubine."* Only on the departure day, the expression "his concubine" reappears (19:9) and it functions as a literary device to fore-shadow her powerless destiny.

If the father-in-law and his son-in-law are put in oppositional rela-tionship, how should we understand the father-in-law's hospitality? The hospitality is extraordinarily bountiful and it looks to be intentional rather than simply customary. Although the two men eat and drink together at the same table, they seem to conceive different thoughts. While the Levite wants to go back to his house with his concubine, his father-in-law makes him stay longer. The father's good treatment of his son-in-law may be under-stood as a protective measure for his daughter,[3] reflecting the father's wish for his son-in-law: be nice to her. Though the space does not allow to intro-duce individual cases of "comfort women," when we remember them, the father's behavior here resembles Korean parents' desperate attempts to hide and save their daughters from being caught by the Japanese soldiers.

Tension and threat are escalating as the narrative unfolds. In the second hospitality scene, the Levite and his company are taken in by an old man at Gibeah. Their rest is interrupted by the men of the city who ask to bring out the Levite to have intercourse with him. The old man offers, "Here are my virgin daughter and his concubine . . . . Ravish them and do whatever you want to them. But against this man do not do such a vile thing" (Judg 19:23). When the mob would not listen to him the Levite turns over his concubine to them. At last, she is gang-raped by the mob through the night. Next morning the Levite finds her lying at the door of the house, with her hands on the threshold. The painful picture of her hands on the threshold invites the reader to witness the unspeakable violence against a powerless human being. Her body is dismembered into twelve pieces by her husband. As Phyllis Trible puts it, "Of all the characters in scripture, she is the least . . . . Captured, betrayed, raped, tortured, murdered, dismembered, and scat-tered—this woman is the most sinned against" (80–81).

Overwhelming violence does not stop there. The Israelite alliance asks the Benjaminites to hand over the men of Gibeah to put them to death. As

---

3 Jones-Warsaw (175) suggests that the father was probably seeking some assurances of his daughter's safety. Fewell and Gunn (133) wonder if the father intentionally delays his son-in-law because he was hesitant to send his daughter back to possible mistreatment.

the Benjaminites refuse, a war between the Benjaminites and the alliance breaks out. Chapter 20 describes the war in detail. The Benjaminites lose the war: all women are destroyed (cf. 21:16) and only 600 men survive. Chapter 21 concerns how to get wives for the 600 men. The alliance chooses to kill all the inhabitants of Jabesh-gilead except for 400 virgins. To get 200 more women, the alliance has the Benjaminite men kidnap young women at the Shiloh festival, just as the Levite handed his concubine over to the Benjaminites before in Gibeah. Trible (83) points out rightly that the rape of one woman became the mass rape of 600 and the concubine's incident is used to justify the expansion of violence against women.

The absurdities of the story are found in various ways. First, the characters are thoroughly nameless. In the Bible it is quite unusual for this kind of long narrative not to have a named character. Rather, only an insignificant figure, Phinehas, is named (20:28). Second, the actions of the characters are inconsistent, illogical, and anti-social. The Levite who comes to bring his concubine back and to "speak tenderly to the heart" (19:3) surrenders her to the mob and dismembers her body, and lies to the Israelite assembly about the incident. The old man in Gibeah offers to the mob not only his unmarried daughter, but also his guest's concubine without even consulting with him. The mob at first wants the Levite, but they end up raping the woman. The alliance is eagerly engaged in the war and seems to forget what originally mattered. Third, the subsequent stories are not closely related. The story line flows from the concubine's death to the actual war and to finding brides. At first, the brutal death of the concubine looks like a direct cause of the war. But as soon as the war begins, the incident is never again mentioned. In fact, at the end of the story in chapter 21 the conclusion of the war has nothing to do with the seemingly original cause of the war. That is, as chapters 19 and 20 are related, so chapters 20 and 21 are related, but chapters 19 and 21 are not related.

All these absurdities and ironies serve to signify the implied intention of the story, which condemns violence against women. Although the narrative includes male victims, it is more plausible to contend that the narrative primarily aims to stress victimization of women. The case becomes clearer when we consider the vivid and detailed description of the appalling death of the Levite's concubine.

How, then, does the biblical story illuminate the "comfort women" story and vice versa? The two stories expose a typical relationship between women and war. The following observations are discerned from the confluence of the two.

1. Women were nameless and thus demeaned. "Comfort women" lost their names from the moment of their being taken and were called by numbers like 1, 2, 3. They were sometimes called by an insulting nickname, *Sen-pee*; *Sen*, a derogatory name in Japanese for *Choson*, the former name for

Korea, and *Pee*, probably hard pronunciation for "p" in "prostitution" in English. Not to mention the anonymity of the Benjaminite women, women of Jabesh-gilead, and women at the Shiloh festival, the namelessness of the Levite's wife, a main figure of the story, is a way of silencing and demeaning her.

2. Women were treated as "things" which have genitals. The Japanese arrested women who were not married. What most "comfort women" had to do was to "service" the Japanese soldiers until the women's sexual organs were swollen, torn and bleeding. In the treatment of women at Jabesh-gilead the yardstick for choosing women to keep alive or to kill was virginity. Those "women who have lain with men" were massacred. The other women were made brides of the Benjaminites.

3. Women were victims of state-organized rape and extravagant violence. The violence in both cases was systematic and collective. Although Japan insists that "comfort stations" were privately run, documents, witnesses, and ex-officers whose consciences are burdened keep coming up. In the biblical story, killing, kidnapping, and rape (through forced marriage) of women were ordered by the alliance. These state- and alliance-organized rapes constitute genocide. The massive rape of Korean women reveals Japanese intention of defiling Korean women and thus destroying their power to reproduce Korean children. The Israelite alliance destroyed the Benjaminite men, women, and children altogether except 600 men. The tribe was about to disappear. These are parallel examples of attempted genocide.

4. Women were victims of wars which were derived from tribal/national and male conflicts/interests. It is redundant to say the "comfort women" system was a result of wars which interested Japanese imperialists. In the biblical story the exact cause of the war was in question. At first, the abuse of the Levite's concubine looks like the direct cause of the war. But we need to note that the narrative reflects conflict among tribes in the formative period of early Israel.[4] Once the war broke out, neither the incident of the concubine was mentioned again, nor did the resolution or conclusion of the war have anything to do with her. Thus, the Levite's concubine was a victim of tribal conflicts which had already been going on.

5. Women were gifts and scapegoats. "Comfort women" were official gifts from the Japanese Emperor to "comfort" the soldiers who were "patriotically fighting for their country to liberate Asian peoples." "Comfort women" were on the list of military supplies and were shipped with the munitions. Similarly, the Levite handed over his concubine to the mob of the town to save himself. She was a dispensable commodity, used to solve an annoyance between males. Women of Jabesh-gilead and Shiloh can be con-

---

4 Niditch (107) points out that the woman functions as a catalyst for war to solve conflicts between men.

sidered as gifts to the Benjaminite soldiers although the narrative disguises this reality with the concern about the extinction of the tribe.

6. Victimized women were forgotten with no comfort. To the women who were used to "comfort" men or to resolve conflict between males there is no comfort. Far from apology and compensation from the Japanese government and understanding and support from Korean people, "comfort women" have been kept secret in modern history. The women in Judges 19–21 have been neglected in the long history of biblical interpretations and sermons. Only recently feminist scholars started giving new light to the story.

C. Han: A Hermeneutical Clue [5]

I believe that a Korean word, *han,* is the most appropriate psychological term to make a connection between "comfort women" and women in Judges 19–21. Although the Koreans commonly call themselves the people of *han,* it is *Minjung* theologians[6] in the 1970s that first utilized the term in theology. *Han* is understood as "the suppressed, amassed and condensed experience of oppression caused by mischief or misfortunes so that it forms a kind of 'lump' in one's spirit" (Suh: 65). Or, it is "a sense of unresolved resentment against injustice suffered, a sense of helplessness because of the overwhelming odds against, a feeling of total abandonment . . ., a feeling of acute pain and sorrow in one's guts and bowels making the whole body writhe and wiggle, and an obstinate urge to take 'revenge' and to right the wrong all these constitute."[7]

I venture to say that *han* represents almost exclusively women's feelings, even though the definitions of theologians and psychiatrists do not attribute a specific gender connotation to the term. While the term can still be applied to men, few idioms about *han* are related to them. There are expressions in Korean like "a woman who has so much *han* inside," "*han* laden woman," and "if a woman conceives *han,* even in the midst of Summer it congeals to frost." There is no such saying about men's *han.*

What about, then, the *han* of comfort women and biblical women? "Comfort women" have been forced to be silent for fifty years. Several brave "comfort women" (they are now called "*Jungshindae* grandmas") started speaking out. Their first utterances were "we have so much *han* in our deepest hearts" and "we have lived lives which were filled with *han.*"

Women in Judges 19–21 can also be called "women who have so much *han* inside." First, the unnamed woman in Judges 19 was a concubine, a

---

5 For extensive studies on *han,* see Lee and Park.

6 *Minjung* theology of Korea is compatible with liberation theology of Latin America. Although *Minjung* theologians tend to avoid giving an exact definition of 'Minjung,' it roughly means 'mass of people in oppressive situation.'

7 This is Hyun Young Hak's definition and is requoted from Chung (42).

secondary wife, who had limited rights (Steinberg: 15–17). Second, she was turned over by her husband to the gangs to be raped, an unbearable betrayal. The betrayal is shockingly intensified by the husband's cutting up of her body into twelve pieces. It means double contamination against her body and thus double *han*. Third, she was gang-raped through the night. In the patriarchal culture which teaches women to keep their chastity as their life, gang-rape denotes multiple killings over one woman. Fourth, she was never properly buried, nor consoled. As Korean folk tales tell, her soul would be restlessly wandering until it is consoled. Fifth, innumerable women in Judges 20 and 21 were targeted and destroy. All women of Jabesh-gilead except 400 women were murdered because of the fault of the men of their city (not attending the assembly). All the women who ever slept with men (the Bible does not say how it was figured out) were killed; the 400 women of Jabesh-gilead who never "knew" men were taken and became wives of strangers, that is, were raped; 200 young women at the Shiloh festival were also taken and raped. All these women have become souls who are wandering between the world beyond and this world with absolute despair and solitude until they are consoled.

The biblical women and "comfort women" are victims of imperialism, militarism, racism, and patriarchy. The biblical women truly are the "comfort women" who were kidnapped without having a clue what would happen to them and were humiliated in confined environments. Like present day "comfort women," the biblical women are our sisters who are still raped and battered today. As Trible (87) claims, "to take to heart this ancient story is to confess its present reality."

III. CONCLUSION: TOWARD THE RESOLUTION OF HAN

The resolution of *han* depends on the consolation of the *han*-laden women. I believe that the task of *han*-resolution of the biblical women can only begin from our repentance for ignoring them, to new and more appropriate interpretations of their stories, as exemplified in the work of Trible and other feminist scholars, in new sermons, in specific rituals, and in ways which will become apparent.

The resolution of the *han* of "comfort women" can also begin from our repentance for neglecting them. War criminals must be found and punished. Although the Japanese government finally accepted their crime recently after its long denial, they still neglect the responsibility of compensation for the victims.

In the Fall of 1992, a twenty-six-year-old Korean woman named Kum-i Yun was murdered by an American soldier in a city of Korea. She was found dead in a room filled with much chemical detergent used as an attempt to conceal criminal evidence. She had been mutilated, a broken Coca-Cola bottle in her vagina, twelve inches of an umbrella stick in her anus, and bruises all over her body. What the Israelites shouted at the news of the dismembered concubine in the ancient day becomes our cry today: "Has this ever happened since the day the Israelites came up from the land of Egypt until this day?" (Judg 19:30). We say, "Yes, and it must stop!"

As long as women are being victimized like Ms. Yun, women of today cannot be satisfied by only reinterpreting the Bible, correcting the history, and receiving reparation. Although our repentance and attempt not to forget the past aim to let it happen never again, our enemy is much stronger than us. The deep-seated diseases like militarism, imperialism, and patriarchy are all over in the world and our sisters are still suffering from them. Our attempt to resolve *han* must continue and so must our fights to prevent all evil powers from causing *han*. The biblical story and the story of Korean "comfort women" compel us to work together with women around the world to end violence against women. Only then will the spirit of *han* recede from the world and the spirit of peace and justice prevail.

WORKS CONSULTED

Bal, Mieke
    1988   *Death & Dissymmetry: The Politics of Coherence in the Book of Judges.* Chicago: University of Chicago Press.

Chung, Hyun Kyung
    1990   *Struggle to Be the Sun Again.* Maryknoll, NY: Orbis.

Fewell, Danna Nolan and David M. Gunn
    1993   *Gender, Power, & Promise: The Subject of the Bible's First Story.* Nashville: Abingdon.

Jones-Warsaw, Koala
    1993   "Toward a Womanist Hermeneutic: A Reading of Judges 19–21." Pp. 172–86 in *A Feminist Companion to Judges.* Ed. A. Brenner. Sheffield: Sheffield Academic.

Korean Council for the Women Drafted for Sexual Service by Japan
    1992a   *Jungshindae Issue Materials I.* Seoul.

    1992b   *Jungshindae Issue Materials II.* Seoul.

Lasine, Stuart
    1984   "Guest and Host in Judges 19: Lot's Hospitality in an Inverted World." *JSOT* 29:37–59.

Lee, Jae Hoon
    1994   *The Exploration of the Inner Wounds—Han.* Atlanta: Scholars.

Niditch, Susan
  1993   *War in the Hebrew Bible: A Study in the Ethics of Violence.* New York: Oxford University Press.

Park, Andrew Sung
  1993   *The Wounded Heart of God: The Asian Concept of Han and the Christian Doctrine of Sin.* Nashville: Abingdon.

Steinberg, Naomi
  1993   *Kinship and Marriage in Genesis: A Household Economics Perspective.* Minneapolis: Fortress.

Suh, Nam Dong
  1981   "Toward a Theology of Han." Pp. 51–66 in *Minjung Theology: People as the Subject of History.* Ed. Yong Bock Kim. Singapore: CTC-CCA.

Trible, Phyllis
  1984   *Texts of Terror: Literary-Feminist Readings of Biblical Narratives.* Philadelphia: Fortress.

Yee, Gale A.
  1995   "Ideological Criticism: Judges 17–21 and the Dismembered Body." Pp. 146–70 in *Judges and Method: New Approaches in Biblical Studies.* Ed. Gale A. Yee. Minneapolis: Fortress.

Returning Home: The Inspiration of the Role Dedifferentiation[1] in the Book of Ruth for Taiwanese Women

Julie L. C. Chu

ABSTRACT

This essay outlines the process of how women in the book of Ruth come to value their own sex and, thereby, reduce the conflicts between mothers and daughters-in-law. It further illustrates its point with the Taiwanese example of present-day mother/daughter-in-law conflicts and gives hope for partnership between these two traditional adversarial roles.

Even today, Taiwanese soap operas still often portray the conflict between mother-in-law and daughter-in-law. In order to capture the loyalty of one man, a husband or a son, these two women become enemies. Although this situation is not so serious as in earlier generations, in real life mothers and daughters-in-law can seldom develop close friendships. This sad fact is probably due to their "role differentiation"—the mother should rely on the son whom she nurtured so hard and the wife should be the husband's only loved woman. Women are made for men, either for being a wife or for being a mother. Women lose their own identity as human beings created in the image of God.

The book of Ruth in the Old Testament gives us a different look at the roles of women and the relationship between mother-in-law and daughter-in-law. It is a book with women's points of view: Naomi demanded that her daughters-in-law go back each to her "mother's" house[2] to find security (place of resting, cf. 1:9; 3:1, rather than the male point of bestowing a name for the family, cf. 4:11); Orpah and Ruth themselves chose different directions for their future (1:14, 16–18); the women of Bethlehem gave the new-born baby a name and praised the value of Naomi's daughter-in-law as better than "seven sons" (4:15). No wonder van Dijk-Hemmes thinks that the book

---

1 This term is borrowed from Berquist (22–37). Since this is a sociological rather than biblical term, I quote Berquist's definition, which is also accepted by sociologist Edward Tiryakian: "the undoing of prior patterns and role definitions, resulting in a condition of less structure." Cf. p. 24. My emphasis on the meaning of this term is to redefine the restrictions for gender and to liberate the traditional patriarchal value of women.

2 According to Trible (169), "mother's house" here could have two explanations: (1) mother-in-law opposes mother, (2) females are radically separated from all males.

of Ruth is from the "women's culture" and a narration from the female perspective (134–39).[3]

Among the three main characters (Naomi, Ruth, and Boaz), two-thirds of them are females. Except for Boaz, all the men in this book are "non-persons,"[4] but three women, including Orpah who speaks only in 1:10, are persons. The beginning (1:6) and the ending (4:17) of the story both focus upon Naomi. Females are no doubt the center of this book. They are miserable widows indeed but they passed the constrictions of their gender and struggled actively for survival and salvation instead of waiting for the males to rescue them. Their role dedifferentiation begins with their consciousness of identifying their own value. These are things extremely important for women today and for Taiwanese women in particular.

I. WOMEN SHOULD STRUGGLE ACTIVELY FOR HOPE AND SALVATION.

The three widows faced a hopeless situation, loss of husbands and sons, yet they made different decisions for their future. Naomi opened her ears to listen to the news from her home town (1:6), and based on this she determined to return. Orpah chose to go back to her own home after Naomi's persuasion.[5] Ruth, however, insisted on following Naomi. They made different choices, yet the choices were their own.

In chapters two and three Ruth actively requested permission from Naomi to glean among the ears of the grain and Naomi initiated the plan for finding security for Ruth, and they both pressed to make Boaz a redeemer and to perform his levirate duty. The cooperation between mother and daughter-in-law replaced the threat of death with the promise of life (Gottwald: 555).

Ruth's performance was even more impressive. She left her homeland, people, and parents' house to go to a place where she had never been. Her faith was much stronger than that of Abraham,[6] the father of faith, who started to a new destination because of God's promise (Gen 12:1–4). Without a promise from the Divine, neither with approval of her mother-in-

---

3 Hubbard (23–24) gives the opinion that the author of this book is a female. Bledstein (132–33) even proposes that David's daughter, Ruth's great-great-granddaughter, Tamar, could be the one who wrote this book.

4 According to the criterion of literary criticism, characters who both speak and have names are "persons," otherwise they belong to the category of "non-persons."

5 From Trible's rhetorical analysis of 1:9b, 14, first Naomi (a) kissed (b) her daughters-in-law (c) while in the end "Orpah (c') kissed (b') her mother-in-law (a') but Ruth (c') clung (b') to her (a'). The change from abc to c'b'a' shows that Naomi's suggestion did not work out because Ruth and Orpah made their own judgment (171).

6 Trible: 173. Trible thinks that Ruth's decision is the most radical one in all the memories of Israel. Levine (80) also makes comparison between Ruth and Abraham.

law,[7] Ruth was still determined to identify with Naomi by accepting Naomi's place, people, and God (1:16–17). When they came to Bethlehem, Naomi complained of coming back "empty" (1:21) and the women who received her did not say a word about Ruth. Disregarded by the others, Ruth did not disregard herself, and she took the responsibility of supporting the family by gleaning.

In her first dialogue with Boaz, she prolonged the conversation by asking him, "Why have I found favor in your sight, that you should take notice of me, when I am a foreigner?" (2:10). Naomi told Ruth that "he will tell you what to do" (3:4); but Boaz could hardly recognize Ruth and said, "Who are you?" Ruth cunningly asked him to spread his cloak over her (3:9). Although we do not know, it may be possible that she surpassed the limitation for her sex by dominating the dialogue.

It is also very possible that only men could initiate the idea of leaving the country for a better land, since in ancient Israel unmarried women were "under the authority" of their fathers and married women should listen to their husbands (de Vaux: 26). Ruth broke the rule for her sex and found a new future in a strange land. These two women struggled together for themselves actively and eventually brought new hope not only for themselves but also for the whole family.

II. FEMINIST CONSCIOUSNESS MAKES WOMEN CLARIFY THEIR OWN VALUE.

Women's chances of working or being educated in human history are mostly in war[8] or turmoil. Such sad backgrounds for the liberation and freedom of women come at a high price. The women's situation in the book of Ruth is similar. Naomi left Bethlehem with Elimelech because of famine, and later all the men in her family died. These disasters definitely gave her another understanding of life. Laffey (210) thinks that the events women face would bring reflection and adjustment of ideology, and their language would change. Female experience is the basis for consciousness-awakening, and this insight made Naomi and Ruth change.

Naomi's use of "mother's house" (1:8) could show her female consciousness. In the Bible "father's house" is more often used, and the context of "mother's house" is often related to marriage.[9] Naomi's language and action proved her new insight, that is, women should stand up and make their own decision.

---

7 Cf. Ruth 1:15 where Naomi said: "Return after your sister-in-law." This shows her disagreement with the decision of Ruth. Levine (80) thinks that Naomi's silence after Ruth's speech (1:16–18) shows that "Naomi never acknowledges her daughter-in-law's fidelity."

8 Berquist (24–26) thinks such an abnormal situation provides room for a role dedifferentiation.

9 Cf. Gen 24:28; Song of Songs 3:4; 8:2; and Levine: 80.

Ruth gave up the hope of finding security in a husband and of living in her own country, and she put this resolution into action by following Naomi. She chose a woman rather than a man as the support of life and gleaned in the field actively (2:2) to support the family on her own. Her liberation is not only about gender but also about class and nationality, since she dared to come to Judah, where the people were not friendly towards Moabites (cf. Deut 23:3). By showing kindness to Naomi, Ruth finally won the respect of Boaz (2:11 and 3:11) and of the women in Bethlehem (4:15).

III. WOMEN AND MEN SUBVERT PATRIARCHY AND AFFIRM THE VALUE OF WOMEN.

Women subverted the traditional patriarchy because of their female consciousness. When the women of Bethlehem greeted Naomi on her arrival, the only words they said were "Is this Naomi?" (1:19), and later they were silent to Naomi's complaining response (1:20–21).

Ruth 4:14–15 is such a contrast to their former dialogue. Naomi said nothing this time and the women praised the Lord joyfully.[10] They affirmed the new-born boy as a "restorer" and "nourisher" of Naomi (4:15). In other words, he was the relative of the living, rather than the one who conveyed the name for the dead (men) (4:11). The women's viewpoint is different from the elders' at the gate (4:11–12). These women spoke with their own voice because they had undergone role dedifferentiation.

They broke through the restrictions of gender and this liberation along with Ruth's good deeds made them see the worth of Ruth which they did not perceive at Naomi's arrival. Finally they understood the value of this Moabite daughter-in-law, praising her as worth "more than seven sons" (4:15) to Naomi. Seven sons! Seven is the number for perfection, and sons are the most precious in a patriarchal society. Their appreciation was really saying that no matter how many and how perfect, sons were no better than Ruth. The women's judgement was liberated from nationality, class, and most of all, gender. Their change was emancipating to Ruth and to themselves, too. By affirming Ruth's value, they assured their own value as females.

The consciousness-awakening in the book of Ruth was not only from the women's side; the man also changed his viewpoint. Boaz also affirmed Ruth's value by claiming her to be "worthy" (3:11), and thus recognized Ruth's status as equal with his own, since the narrator of this book previously described Boaz as "worthy" (2:1).[11] Ruth became a truly equal partner

---

[10] Their joyful song is an echo of the song of Deborah (Judg 5) and the song of Miriam (Exod 15:20–21).

[11] Although English or Mandarin translation uses different words in these verses, the Hebrew vocabulary in the original text is exactly the same.

to Boaz, although she belonged to the "second sex" in the patriarchal stereotype at that time.

This is a journey of returning for Naomi, Ruth, Boaz, the women of Bethlehem, and also, for the daughters-in-law and mothers-in-law in Taiwan. Naomi finally made her own decision for herself to return to her home town. Orpah and Ruth also made up their own minds to travel in opposite directions. Ruth chose to accompany and to be a partner with Naomi. In her touching confessions she showed her determination to confess Naomi's God and people as hers. For her, it was a long way home since people there were not friendly to Moabites.

Ruth was not so intimidated by the unfriendliness at all. She tried her best to identify herself as a Jew by practicing her promise to Naomi (1:16–17) and by gleaning in the field according to the custom. Ruth's determination probably encouraged Naomi and made her initiate the daring plan for their future (3:1). Comparing this plan to the complaint in 1:13, 20–21, we know that Naomi has returned to confidence in life, and even to trust in God again. Naomi and Ruth, with the help of God who guided Boaz to lie down "at the end of the heap of grain" (3:7) and awoke Boaz in the middle of the night (3:8), found the redeemer and levirate successfully.

Ruth finally returned—not only to the security of a husband, but also to a new identity. She was accepted by Boaz, blessed by the elders, and praised by the women. Bethlehem was no longer a foreign land; this was a new home for her. The God of Israel abundantly rewarded her deeds and she was even considered one among the "great mothers of Israel."[12] Boaz and the women returned[13] because of recognizing the true value of females.

Mothers and daughters-in-law in Taiwan are still very differentiated by their sex and roles, that is, they overemphasize their roles and responsibilities as mothers and wives to the degree that they forget that they themselves are also important subjects. A mother is expected to take care of her son for his entire life, thus she sometimes does not provide enough private space for the new couple.[14] Even though in Taiwan today not all young couples must live

---

12 The people and elders in the gate put her among Rachel, Leah, and Tamar. Cf. 4:11–12.

13 Recognizing the value of women could be a "turning" of point of view. However, I think that the value of women comes from God's creation since women also share God's own image (Gen 1:27). Thus the term "returning" emphasizes that people's values in Ruth finally travel back to the original view of creation. The effect of the patriarchal society makes us over-accentuate males. Otherwise, equality would be the prototype.

14 This is still a serious issue focused by the soap operas and novels. One of my friend's personal experiences might help readers of other than Taiwanese or Oriental background understand this seriousness. She is a psychiatrist and also a director in a teaching hospital. Her husband insisted on giving her mother-in-law the key of their new apartment. The mother-in-law would come in without knocking and break into her bedroom no matter what my friend was doing. She felt violated and was angry as well as upset. Even an intellectual like her could not protect her privacy in marriage, let alone the lower-class women.

with their parents, the mother-in-law still has society's approval to direct and check the new couple's affairs.[15]

And because the present mothers-in-law were treated comparatively worse by their own mothers-in-law decades ago, they think the daughters-in-law today are more fortunate, which is also very true. This kind of attitude helps generate conflict and jealousy. Daughters-in-law today have more opportunities for education and are more open to modern thought, and sometimes they do not really respect their mothers-in-law. These antipathies create gaps and even hatred between them. Actually the society influences the importance of their sex roles. They are seriously differentiated. If the case of Naomi and Ruth happened in Taiwan or China, neighbors and relatives might think that either the daughters-in-law were responsible for the men's deaths or the men died because of the unfortunate women in the family. In Taiwanese culture, women are usually blamed for the misfortunes of the family[16] to rationalize tragedies that cannot be understood.

Placing emphasis only on sons who can continue the family name creates a great barrier for women to recognize their own value. The neighbor women in the book of Ruth, even though they rejoiced over the new-born boy, also obviously highlighted Ruth's value. "Better than seven sons" is their comment about Naomi's loving and faithful daughter-in-law. For them, women's worth was not only bearing sons. Women themselves are very valuable. If Taiwanese people could learn this positive attitude toward females, mothers and daughters-in-law would cherish their own sex and be more respectful to each other; this would reduce the role conflicts.

Taiwanese mothers-in-law and daughters-in-law both need to return to the order of Creation, just like the males and females in the book of Ruth. With self-confidence, they will not try to control their sons or husbands to show their own value because they themselves are very precious indeed. With gender consciousness-awakening, mothers-in-law and daughters-in-law will respect their own sex which is from God and will love each other. Women will return to the affirmation of their own sex, to the assurance of female value, and to the beautiful friendship of partners.[17]

---

15 Mothers-in-law can also control the usage of money, criticize the cleaning of the house, and direct the household. Sometimes the mother-in-law could even be the major reason for a couple's divorce.

16 There is a special Mandarin and Taiwanese verb *khek* (Taiwanese sound translation) for this. The meaning is "to cause to death". This kind of thought—that women bear the responsibility for the misfortune of the family, or women "killed the dead"—is so deep that it even affects people today. I went to a funeral on October 7, 1996. Before the dead man was buried, his wife could no longer control herself and cried her husband's name saying: "I did not do anything wrong. People said you died because of me. Please don't go away." Widows are doubly hurt, first by the death of their family members, and second, by people's prejudice.

17 Before concluding this article, I must make one thing clear. Not all Taiwanese mothers-in-law are a problem to their daughters-in-law. Take myself for example, my mother-in-law

WORKS CONSULTED

Berquist, Jon L.
1993   "Role Dedifferentiation in the Book of Ruth." *JSOT* 57:23–37.

Bledstein, Adrien J.
1993   "Female Companionships: If Ruth Were Written by a Woman . . ."
        Pp. 116–33 in *A Feminist Companion to Ruth*. Ed. Athalya Brenner.
        Sheffield: Sheffield Academic.

De Vaux, Roland
1984   "The Typical Israelite Marriage." Pp. 26–29 in *Ancient Israel: Its Life and
        Institutions*. Trans. John McHugh. London: Darton, Longman & Todd.

Gottwald, Norman K.
1987   *The Hebrew Bible: A Socio-Literary Introdubtion*. Philadelphia: Fortress.

Hubbard, Robert L., Jr.
1991   *The Book of Ruth*. Grand Rapids: Eerdmans.

Laffey, Alice L.
1988   "Women's Story: Ruth, Naomi, and Orpah." Pp. 205–10 in *An Introduc-
        tion to the Old Testament. A Feminist Perspective*. Philadelphia: Fortress.

Levine, Amy-Jill
1992   "Ruth." Pp. 78–84 in *The Women's Bible Commentary*. Ed. Carol A.
        Newsom and Sharon H. Ringe. Louisville: Westminster/John Knox.

Trible, Phyllis
1978   "A Human Comedy." Pp. 166–99 in *God and the Rhetoric of Sexuality*.
        Philadelphia: Fortress.

Van Dijk-Hemmes, Fokkelien
1993   "Ruth: A Product of Women's Culture?" Pp. 134–39 in *A Feminist Com-
        panion to Ruth*. Ed. Athalya Brenner. Sheffield: Sheffield Academic.

encouraged me to become further equipped in theology after my marriage. The thought that training a woman is a waste never occurred to her. She is always so supportive and generous that my friends all envy me. This is why I am especially interested in the problem between mothers and daughters-in law. I hope that someday no Taiwanese daughters-in-law will envy me because they themselves also will have wonderful mothers-in-law.

Proverbs 31:10–31 in a South African Context: A Reading for the Liberation of African (Northern Sotho) Women

Madipoane Masenya
University of South Africa

ABSTRACT

The context of readers shapes the way they read the Bible. In a South African setting, an African (Northern Sotho) woman's context is characterised by a variety of oppressive forces like post-apartheid racism, sexism, classism, and oppressive elements of the African culture. A short survey of these factors is given. With reference to this context, the author re-reads Proverbs 31:10–31 from a *Bosadi* (Womanhood) perspective, a woman's liberation perspective which is committed, amongst other things, to the African-ness of an African–South African woman.

INTRODUCTION

Handling the Christian Bible, which is designated by many Black South Africans (particularly the youth) as a White man's book, in post-apartheid South Africa is not always easy. Such a designation is understandable in the light of how some missionaries and the previous apartheid government abused the Bible in order to serve their own interests. The Bible was used, among other things, to subordinate non-White people, thus confirming what these abusers of the Bible read into it, namely that Blacks were destined by God to be the servants of the Whites.

Despite this negative situation, there are still many Black South Africans (in particular women) who have interest in the Bible and regard it as a norm for their lives. Indeed the majority of Church-going people among Africans (Northern Sothos)[1] in South Africa are women. Despite this, the Christian Church fails to give them authority to interpret the Bible in the churches. The Bible has been interpreted (and this is still the case) by men from a male

---

[1] Northern Sotho people form part of the many African tribes (e.g. Zulus, Vendas, Vha-Tsonga) in the country. In this paper, the word African will refer primarily to the indigenous peoples of South Africa without making claims for all Africans, though I recognize that there are some significant commonalities. I prefer to focus on the Northern Sotho group (as a sample representing all the other African tribes in the country), as I belong to this group.

perspective. Such an unfortunate state of affairs may not be allowed to continue in the so-called 'non-sexist,' post-apartheid South Africa, and not in the church. The latter, I would argue, is supposed to exemplify a situation of justice because the God portrayed in the Bible, in my view, identifies with the marginalised sections of society.

My intention in this paper is to read Proverbs 31:10–31 from the perspective of the liberation of African women. In my Christian context, this paean is favoured as a text exemplifying the qualities of a good Christian woman. The text is read literally without due consideration of, among other things, the context that produced it or the terminology used in the Hebrew text. Many Black people (particularly women) with their past history of deprivation and poverty do not have access to critical biblical scholarship. Some cannot even read.

My main intention in re-reading this poem in an African (Northern Sotho) context is to see if indeed the woman who is pictured as worthy can offer liberating possibilities for the many oppressed women who live in my context. Before I engage in this, however, I will give a brief picture of the context of an African woman in South Africa. The point of departure in this paper is that people's experiences, in one way or other, shape the way they read the Bible. It thus becomes essential to get a portrait of the various factors impacting the life of an African (Northern Sotho) woman in South Africa to see how these shape her experiences and, ultimately, how the latter shape her reading of the Bible.

The Context of an African Woman in South Africa

There are a number of different factors affecting the lives of African women in our country. Four important ones are: racism, classism, sexism and the African culture. In this paper, I shall focus mainly on the last three, because these three factors or oppressive elements, even in post-apartheid South Africa, still shape the lives of many African women to a great extent. I should hasten to argue that even the first one, that is racism, is still alive in our country, though comparatively speaking, the situation has now improved. African women thus know the inter-relatedness of these factors, and racism has been significant in the expression of these forces. For example, in the apartheid era, what counted most was one's race. The country's resources were distributed accordingly. Africans, for example, were allocated infertile pieces of land and poor educational facilities. One was regarded as less than human due to the colour of one's skin. Such a notion of the 'chosenness' of the other 'superior' race versus the 'inferiority' of the Black race, whose destiny was viewed as being that of servitude to others, dominated centuries of colonial rule in South Africa. It is no wonder that even in the post-colonial, post-apartheid South Africa, such a mentality is still or will still prevail in the minds of many white people.

1. Classism

I have already noted that racism in apartheid South Africa determined the distribution of the land's resources. Elsewhere I have argued: "Due to this political, social and economic deprivation, Blacks could only qualify as the have-nots and thus as members of a lower class" (Masenya: 37). The present situation in the country of the many poverty-stricken Black families bears witness to this statement. African women always find themselves at the bottom of the *kyriarchal* ladder.

I prefer the term *kyriarchy* (domination by the master or lord) to patriarchy (domination by the father), as the former includes several forms of oppressions, such as racism, classism and sexism, while patriarchy basically focuses on sexism (Schüssler Fiorenza: 114–18). One example will suffice: The apartheid, *kyriarchal* South Africa advantaged African men over African women (cf. educational and job opportunities); hence the many illiterate African women today. Such women, unlike some of us, do not have the privilege of reading the Bible. For such women survival in the midst of homelessness, malnutrition, and hunger is viewed as an answer to prayers directed to God who hears and answers prayers.

2. African Culture

Another form of oppression affecting the life of an African woman is some aspects of the patriarchal African culture. By African culture I refer to the customary beliefs, social forms, and material traits of Africans in South Africa. There is a tendency among some black feminist scholars to portray the African culture in a positive light with regard to its treatment of women while blaming it all on colonialism and its capitalist system (Steady; Rivkin). I would argue that the latter only served to reinforce the patriarchy inherent in the African culture. The words of Ramodibe (15) are worthy of note in this regard:

> African tradition and culture present themselves to women as an oppressive system. It has a male-domineering factor. It is a patriarchal system. This oppressive patriarchal system was found in South Africa even before whites came with their Western capitalist culture.

It is an indisputable fact that African culture, like all other patriarchal cultures, has a low view of women. A few examples will suffice: A man may be described with contempt as a woman, as in the following sentence: *O no ba mosadi* "You are just a woman," particularly when he behaves sheepishly. A married woman is valued mainly as a bearer of children, particularly sons. Little girls are already viewed in terms of their future marriages. In such settings, marriage becomes an idol. Hence the fact that women may rather opt for polygyny than for celibate lives. While marriage is good, it should not be idolized, particularly in Christian settings (cf. 1 Cor 7:25ff.). Such a low view of women affects their self-esteem and self-identity. Such an identity, in one way or another, I suggest, will affect one's reading of the Bible.

3. Sexism

Despite the popular slogan that proclaims a "non-racist, non-sexist South Africa,"[2] sexism is quite at home in post-apartheid South Africa, particularly in African women's settings (Mosala: 129–33). This sexism is, in part at least, a consequence of apartheid economics interacting with traditional views about women's and men's roles.

With the introduction of the apartheid South African capitalistic economy, there emerged a *sharp* division between the public and the private spheres. The former was viewed as belonging to men, with African men being exploited, while the latter was viewed as belonging to women—and, disturbingly, tended to be despised—a sphere of domesticity and family life. The unfortunate result is that the sphere dealing with the family[3] came to be looked down upon. That was not the case, however, in pre-colonial South Africa. The economy of the household has always formed part of the home. The division of the public versus the private sphere was thus slim. Both men and women worked together in the economy of the family. In South Africa, the division between the two spheres only became significant with the introduction of capitalist economy by colonialists. A new definition of labour as a way of earning money was introduced. As a result, Western wages (money) were more esteemed than African wages (crops, cattle, etc.). Hence, work that was performed in the public sphere (mostly by men) came to be more valued than that done in the private sphere by women. Even the contribution that African women used to make in the agricultural economy of the family was undermined by the capitalistic government as large scale agricultural economy fell into the hands of the powerful few. African women are therefore left with infertile fields which only yield poor crops in their small scale subsistence farming.

---

2 This slogan is commonly used in political circles and was particularly used by politicians in their political campaigns prior to the country's first democratic elections in 1994.

3 I say unfortunate because, for typical Africans, the family, kinship, and clans occupy a central role in their lives.

The diminished value of women's contribution to the economy leaves women with the full burden of household duties but without recognition or reward. The newly married woman faces expectations by her in-laws that may be summarized by the Northern Sotho proverb, *mosadi ke tšhwene o lewa mabogo* (literally "a woman is a baboon, her hands are eaten"). The meaning of the proverb is: A commendable woman is the one who does her household duties effectively and also takes care of her husband (Rakoma: 184). All the hard work of domesticity is to be handled by her.

The church is no exception regarding the discrimination of women on the basis of their sex. Though the churches (both the missionary churches and the African Independent churches) are dominated by women, they are basically not allowed to actualize fully their God-given potential, merely because of their God-given sex.

Given such circumstances, how must the Bible be read to cater for the context of these women? In this paper, I propose an African woman's liberation approach, exemplified by a reading of Proverbs 31:10–31. This approach will take into account the African-ness of an African woman in South Africa. This is necessary in a setting where the African culture has been denigrated. The introduction of Christianity in the country was coupled with the demonization of the African culture and the idolization of the Western one. As a result, even the good elements of the African culture were eroded. With the approach I am proposing, I hope to revive those elements of this culture which elevate the status of women and to criticize the oppressive ones. Such an approach fits in well with the post-apartheid South Africa with its emphasis on the democratic rights of individuals.

I call this concept *bosadi*, from the Northern Sotho word for "womanhood." *Bosadi* comes from the word *mosadi* (woman) and describes what it means to be a woman in a Northern Sotho culture: what ideal womanhood is; what qualities are expected of a woman in this culture. The *bosadi* approach will focus, among other things, on the following:

1. Reviving the positive elements (liberatory aspects) of the African culture regarding women as well as criticising the oppressive elements of this culture. Some aspects of the African culture which this perspective will highlight are worthy of note:
   a. The concept of *ubuntu* (*botho*/humanness), which implies a fundamental respect for human nature as a whole (Teffo: 14). It is a social ethic, a unifying vision enshrined in the Zulu maxim, *umuntu ngumuntu ngabanye* (Northern Sotho version: *motho ke motho ka batho*). The literal meaning of the proverb is: "A human being is a human being because of other human beings." African humanism is typified by the following norms and values: justice; respect for person and property; tolerance;

compassion; sensitivity to the aged, the handicapped and less privileged; reliability; etc.
   b. The concept of *bosadi*—in its emphasis on the family. Where necessary,
   the concept *bosadi* elevates the significance of the family. The latter
   played and still plays a significant role in Africa.
2. Shifting from the traditional approach to the Bible, which embraced it un-
   critically. The present perspective approaches the Bible with suspicion; it
   will question the oppressive elements of the Bible with regard to women
   and revive or harness the liberatory ones.
3. Taking note of the interplay of oppressive forces such as racism, sexism,
   classism and the African culture as factors shaping the way the African
   woman reads the Bible.

AN AFRICAN WOMAN READS PROVERBS 31:10–31

General Orientation to the Text

Proverbs 31:10–31 is the second part of Proverbs 31. It is preceded by an
instruction in vv. 1–9 which is attributed to a foreign woman, the queen
mother of Lemuel, King of Massa. Our paean is an acrostic poem whose
problematic position of closing the whole book makes it difficult to read. I
refer to the poem's position at the end of the book as being problematic because of the nature of the book as a whole, as comprised of a variety of main
sections. We may ask, for example, whether 31:10–31 is a fitting conclusion
to the whole book, or whether it is an appendage to the book.

Indeed, through the years the poem has been interpreted differently by
various male interpreters.[4] It is disturbing to note that little has been done
regarding the reading of this poem from a feminist/women's liberation perspective.[5] It is not my intention in this paper to focus on the debate regarding
the various interpretations enjoyed by this paean over the years. The fact that
our text is a poem and forms part of the book of Proverbs makes it susceptible to a variety of readings which might be miles away from the intention
of its original authors or redactors. Secondly, it is not always easy to date
the material in the book of Proverbs. For example, in the present text the
poet focuses on the family or the ideal wife in the family. Though Camp
would argue that the family regained power as the locus of authority in the
post-exilic period, family/folk wisdom was already extant in pre-monarchic

---

4 See Wolters for an elaborate treatment of this subject.
5 To my knowledge Claudia Camp seems to be the only feminist scholar in the States who
has put more effort into the re-reading this text. My present presentation will thus focus on her
frequently. I also wish to thank her for the insight she offered me regarding this text during my
short stay in the U.S. (March–June 1995).

Israel. Camp herself maintains that we are not compelled to date the Proverbs poems of chapters 1–9 and 31 in the post-exilic era, for there is a possibility that older works were included in the collection.

Of the interpretations that the poem enjoyed in previous years, two are worthy of note:

1. The poem presents the picture of an ideal Israelite woman. According to this interpretation, the paean does not deal with an historical woman, but presents an idealized picture (Camp, 1985; Bird; Aitken; Crook).
2. The woman portrayed in the piece is wisdom personified. The poem thus presents wisdom in the form of a metaphor, as a woman (McCreesh; Gous).[6]

Camp (1996) supports the first interpretation, but maintains that although the acrostic is highly stylised, it cannot be totally removed from a historical context. In her treatment of the figure of female wisdom (Camp, 1985:12), she has argued that the female figures in the book of Proverbs are not just literary forms; they should be tied to a certain socio-historical setting. She observes:

> Literary and religious forms do not arise and live in a vacuum. People give to these forms meaning which is born of their experience, even as the forms in turn shape that experience. Therefore a full interpretation of the figure of female Wisdom can and should try to describe a possible historical and sociological locus where such a figure could give and receive meaning.

This suggests that though the poet might not have been dealing with a particular human woman in this text, his portrayal of woman could have been based on certain particular observations that Israelite society had about women.

As we read the poem, we do not doubt that the poet relates the practical qualities of a human woman. This is unlike the passages dealing with Woman Wisdom, a metaphorical picture of woman in Proverbs 1–9, in which the reader can clearly observe the metaphorical usage of language. For these reasons, I differ with scholars like McCreesh and Gous who see the Woman of Worth of Proverbs 31:10–31 as Wisdom personified.That should not imply that I do not see close similarities between this poem and those dealing with Woman Wisdom in Proverbs 1–9. Their apparent similarities do not however convince me that the אשת חיל is Woman Wisdom.

In Proverbs 31:10–31 the poet has given us an idealised picture of a woman. This is surely not a real woman; it is an ideal. Aitken notes:

---

6 For an elaborate treatment, see McCreesh; cf. Camp, 1985.

> So, while there are "ordinary points" in the portrait that should commend
> themselves to any housewife, above all that she "fears the Lord"—as a
> whole it cannot be read as a kind of blueprint of the ideal Israelite house-
> wife—either for men to measure their wives against or for their wives to.
> (158)

I would, however, differ with Aitken's assertion that the ideal woman portrayed here was not meant to be emulated. I think that the reason for this
portrayal, and also for the inclusion of this piece in the canon, was that this
ideal could be striven for. This striving for an ideal makes sense particularly
in a context where there was an identity crisis, a crisis which according to
some scholars had to do with who the true Jew was (cf. Horsley; Washington;
Eskenazi and Judd). In such a context, men would strive for an ideal or true
Jewish woman who, unlike Woman Stranger, for example, would not cause
disruption to society.

My argument would therefore be that the portrait is not that of a real
woman but an ideal that people (men) had to strive for, an ideal based on
certain expectations which society had about women. This understanding
implies that we are dealing here with a male text addressed to a male audience. As Whybray observes: "Material prosperity and good standing [of men]
in the community go together, and a good wife is necessary for their achieve-
ment" (184; brackets mine). In the same way, Fontaine argues: "As always
in male-centered Scripture, the positive and negative roles of women are
viewed primarily from the perspective of what they provide for the men
involved" (516).

Apart from the male orientation of the paean, one other aspect that arrests my interest as a South African *mosadi* is the class of the text. Fontaine
(108) is right when she argues that "it is clear that when we first hear the
voices of the wise in Proverbs, we are hearing the speech of the artistic elite."
The class of woman portayed in our poem suggests that the readers (young
men of repute who aspire for such a wife) probably come from a higher class.
The אשת חיל is an upper class woman (Fontaine: 516; Waegeman: 101; Mc-
Creesh: 31). Fontaine notes that the family unit pictured in Proverbs 31:10–31
is an elite one in keeping with the social background and goals of the sages.

The difficult question is: How did the women of the time react to a
text such as this one? Did they find it to be liberative or demeaning? The
latter is clearly one of the concerns of modern women readers. I am not sure
if the Jewish women of the time (those who lived in early post-exilic Palestine, in the Achaemenid period) were interested in such questions. It is
difficult to speak on their behalf as they were mostly excluded from the
public social activities of the time. One thing for sure is that the picture
of the woman presented here is not representative of all the women of that
time, for it excludes rural and poor women, for example. Consequently, it
would appear to be a problematic text if read from an African–South African

woman's liberation perspective. A sceptical reader may ask what a poor Northern Sotho woman may benefit from a male elitist text. I wish to argue that though the text does have oppressive elements, it also contains liberative or life-giving elements.

PROVERBS 31:10–31 FROM A BOSADI PERSPECTIVE

Certain expectations that the Jews in the early post-exilic period probably had about women come to light as one reads the poem:

1. Woman as household manager

The key among them appears to be the expectation that the Israelite woman was supposed to be manager of the family. Ancient Israelite women were viewed as managers of the households in which they lived (Camp, 1985: 85). As one reads the paean, it becomes very clear that the אשת חיל is in control of the household (cf. also Meyers: 47–48; Bird: 57). The latter is actually called hers (cf. the Hebrew ביתה, vv.15, 21 and 27). It thus becomes ironic that the author uses the word בעל (master) for husband, though this may make sense in the context of a patriarchal culture. Also noteworthy regarding the relations of the Woman of Worth with her husband is that it is assumed that one of the expected responsibilities of the Israelite wife was to promote the interests of the husband. Her husband is known in the city gate (v. 23), "She does him good, not harm, all the days of her life." While it is good that a wife is supposed to take care of her husband's interests, it would have been unfortunate if such expectations had been one-sided. Such one-sidedness has, in most cases, led to the subordination of women all over the world, the African family in South Africa being no exception.

Some feminist scholars (Camp, 1987:55–56; Brenner: 129) would however see this "sphere of weakness" (private sphere) as actually a source of power. Because of what is done in the private sphere, the husband becomes successful in the public sphere (the gates). Brenner is right when she argues:

> Her voice might indeed be muted within the public culture, she shares a predominantly male culture.This is explained by her sitting at home while her menfolk are passing their time in public places (at the gates). She lives to advance male interests and male well-being. In so doing however, she ultimately subverts the male order by becoming its focal point and essential requisite. (129)

It should however be noted that the אשת חיל is not only confined to the home (household), though the latter, as we will later observe, might not necessarily be problematic if viewed from a *bosadi* perspective. The Woman of Worth is also responsible for the household economy.

This quality of the Woman of Worth reminds one of the Northern Sotho saying: *Lapa ke la mosadi* "the family belongs to a woman." The saying simply means that a woman is expected to take up the full responsibility of the household and all matters pertaining to domesticity. While such a position of responsibility may be empowering for women in that it recognises that they can also manage certain activities, particularly for those women who have no option but to be housewives, it might be dehumanising if it is used as an excuse to confine women to the household. In my view, an outstanding quality of the אשת חיל as it is is portrayed in the present poem is that she is a family woman, she has the interests of her family at heart.

As I have clearly indicated the significance of the family for Africans, it may be expected that this quality of the Woman of Worth may have liberating possibilities for an African woman in South Africa. Being in the family and managing it in our context is, in my view, a position of power due to the following considerations:

a. Due to the migratory policies of the apartheid regime, many African women had to serve and are still serving as both fathers and mothers of families as their husbands had to move to cities to work. The women thus had to display good administrative skills for the smooth running of the family.

b. Remaining at home does not imply that a woman is not making a contribution to the family. Bearing children and nurturing them in cultures that set great store by children, like the Hebraic and the African ones, is not necessarily a position of weakness. It is actually a position of power, because a woman who is more valued or enjoys a higher status is the one who has children. While there is nothing wrong with such an approach in my opinion, it becomes problematic if it is promoted at all costs, for example, if barrenness or having few children is viewed as a genuine ground for divorce. It also becomes problematic, particularly with regard to present day conditions in which more and more women join the public sphere, if nurturing is viewed as a woman's role only.

c. Remaining at home does not necessarily imply that one is not making a living for the family. Many African women operate small business transactions from their homes. They do not necessarily need to go outside home to work. Thus African women in South Africa (cf. also their African-American sisters) have always worked.

By way of concluding this discussion of the quality of the woman as household manager, I would like to argue that anyone (man or woman) who would like to operate from home, which is in my view an important sphere, should not be looked down upon. That person is also making a contribution in that sphere.

2. A Woman Cares for the Needy

Another quality that comes to light as one reads our paean is that of caring for the needy. As noted earlier, a general view among commentators is that the אשת חיל is a rich woman, a woman of the upper class (Bird: 57; Mc-Creesh: 27; McKane: 669). Thus this picture is not representative of all the women of the time. In particular, it does not accommodate poor women. What captures my attention as an African-South African woman is the portrait of a very rich woman who cares for the poor, not just mentioning the need to care for the poor, not just involved in charity work for the poor, but actually extending (שלח) her hands to reach out to them. In apartheid South Africa, one would think of a picture (a rare one I suggest) of a very rich White woman reaching out her hands to the poor of the land.

This caring quality of the Woman of Worth reminds one of the *ubuntu/botho* concept of the African culture. We have already noted that compassion and sensitivity to the less privileged, justice, and tolerance rank among the most pertinent norms and values of this African humanism. What the אשת חיל does, her generosity and care for the needy, reminds one of what used to be the case in the Northern Sotho culture. In a village, for example, an elderly person without children would not be left all by her/himself; young girls would visit to provide them with water, wood, etc. Food could even be prepared for them if they were no longer in a position to do it themselves. African people, like the אשת חיל, are culturally caring and compassionate people. It is just unfortunate that even such good elements of our culture have been lost and are still being eroded in favour of an individualistic Western culture. Hence the need for approaches such as the one advocated here. This quality of caring for the poor reminds African women who happen to belong to better classes to take care of their many poor African sisters.

3. The Woman is Hard Working

The last quality of the אשת חיל that I would like to focus on is that of her industry. The fact that the Woman of Worth manages *all aspects* of a complex household shows that we are here dealing with an industrious woman, a woman who according to verse 27 "does not eat the bread of idleness." The manifold tasks which the Woman of Worth does are, in my view, one of the proofs that this paean presents an idealized picture. No flesh and blood person can perform such tasks with such efficiency. Nevertheless, we may assume that the poet wished to give us a portrait of a hard working woman.

The Northern Sotho proverb, cited above, that likens a woman to a baboon, carries with it the idea that one of the aspects of womanhood in this culture is hard work. Indeed in this context, a woman—particularly a newly married one—is expected to work tirelessly. Industry as a virtue is required of every society, including the South African society. I wish to argue that hard work is not supposed to be confined to women only, as is implied in the above proverb. The quality of the אשת חיל as an industrious woman may be enriching for Northern Sotho women in a context where everybody, and not only women, is expected to work hard. It also becomes enriching in a context where hard work is rewarded. On the other hand, it may be an oppressive quality if only a section of society is expected to work hard and without fair remuneration.

In conclusion I would like to argue that the portrait of the אשת חיל as manager of household, caring for the needy, and industrious, can partially offer liberating possibilities if the text is read from a *bosadi* perspective. It is liberative for some lost aspects of the African culture, like the significance of the family (for all, not only for women) and the significance of industry for people of all races, sexes, and classes in South Africa (including African women who have always worked hard); and the *ubuntu/botho* concept for all can be restored. If Africans can revive and reclaim these good qualities of their culture, they will hopefully regain their self-worth and self-identity as African Christians without the appendage "Westernized" (civilized?).

The portrait of a family (household) that the poet presents in this paean is that of husband and wife, children and servants. Something interesting and also making sense in the light of the patriarchal environment of the poet is that, of all the members of the household of the Woman of Worth, the husband is the one who is foregrounded by the poet (vv. 11, 12, 23, 28). From the picture we are given in this poem we may assume that according to ancient Israelite mentality (and the Northern Sotho one), the ideal family is the one which has man, woman, and children. In real life situations, this is not always the case. With the many political upheavals in our country, many families have been bereft of their menfolk; many African families are single-parented, being managed by women, and some are part and parcel of extended families. Yet in the African community, as I have argued, if there are people who show devotion to church matters, prayer, and Bible study, these are women. Women in these families may not find the picture of the אשת חיל wholly liberating.

I wish to argue that while marriage is good, it should not serve as an institution in which the status of one individual is defined in terms of the other, and it must not be idolized. Furthermore, a family which may not appear ideal according to my standards should not be denigrated, and those who opt for celibacy should not be judged.

WORKS CONSULTED

Aitken, K. T.
    1986   *Proverbs*. Philadelphia: Westminster.

Bird, Phyllis A.
1974   "Images of Women in the Old Testament." Pp. 41–60 in *Religion and Sexism: Images of Woman in the Jewish and Christian Traditions*. Ed. Rosemary R. Ruether. New York: Simon and Schuster.

1995   Personal conversation. Evanston, IL.

Brenner, Athalya
1993.   "An F Voice?" Pp. 113–30 in *On Gendering Texts: Female and Male Voices in the Hebrew Bible*. Eds. Athalya Brenner and Fokkelien van Dijk-Hemmes. Leiden: Brill.

Camp, Claudia V.
1985   *Wisdom and the Feminine in the Book of Proverbs*. Decatur, GA: Almond.

1987   "Woman Wisdom as Root Metaphor." Pp. 45–76 in *The Listening Heart: Essays in Wisdom and the Psalms in Honor of Roland Murphy (O Carm)*. Ed. Kenneth G. Hoglund. Sheffield: JSOT.

1995   Telephone conversation, May 4, 1995.

Crook, Margaret B.
1954   "The Marriageable Maiden of Proverbs 31:10–31." *JNES* 8:137–40.

Eskenazi, Tamara C. and Eleanore P. Judd
1994   "Marriage to a Stranger in Ezra 9–10." Pp. 266–85 in *Second Temple Studies. Vol 2: Temple Community in the Persian Period*. Ed. Tamara C. Eskenazi and Kent H. Richards. Sheffield: JSOT.

Fontaine, Carole R.
1988   "Proverbs." Pp. 495–517 in *Harper's Bible Commentary*. Ed. James L. Mays. San Francisco: Harper and Row.

Fontaine, Carole R.
1993   "Wisdom in Proverbs." Pp. 99–114 in *In Search of Wisdom: Essays in Memory of John G. Gammie*. Ed. Leo G. Perdue et al. Louisville: Westminster/John Knox.

Gous, Ignatius G. P.
1995   "Proverbs 31:10–31—the A to Z of Woman Wisdom." Paper presented at the annual meeting of the Old Testament Society of South Africa. Port Elizabeth.

Horsley, Richard A.
1991   "Empire,Temple and Community—but no Bourgeoisie! A Response to Blenkinsopp and Petersen." Pp. 163–74 in *Second Temple Studies.Vol 1.: Persian Period*. Ed. Philip R. Davies. Sheffield: JSOT.

Masenya, Joyce M.
1994   "Freedom in Bondage: Black Feminist Hermeneutics." *JBTSA* 8:35–48.

McCreesh, Thomas P.
1985   "Wisdom as Wife: Proverbs 31:10–31." *RB* 92:25–46.

McKane, William
1970   *Proverbs: A New Approach*. London: SCM.

Meyers, Carol
1991   "'To Her Mother's House': Considering a Counterpart to the Israelite *Bêt āb.*" Pp. 39–51 in *The Bible and the Politics of Exegesis*. Ed. David Jobling, Peggy L. Day, and Gerald T. Sheppard. Cleveland: Pilgrim.

Mosala, Bennedette I.
1986   "Black Theology and the Struggle of Women in South Africa." Pp. 129–33 in *The Unquestionable Right to Be Free: Black Theology from South Africa*. Ed. Itumeleng J. Mosala and Buti Tlhagale. Braamfontein: Skotaville.

Rakoma, J. R. D.
1971   *Marema-ka-Dika tša Sesotho sa Leboa*. Pretoria: Van Schaik.

Ramodibe, Dorothy
1989   "Woman and Men Building Together the Church in South Africa." Pp. 14–21 in *With Passion and Compassion: Third World Women Doing Theology*. Ed. Virginia Fabella and Mercy A. Oduyoye. Maryknoll: Orbis.

Rivkin, Elizabeth T.
1994   "The Black Woman in South Africa." Pp. 215–29 in *The Black Woman Cross-culturally*. Ed. Filomina C. Steady. Rochester, VT: Schenkman.

Steady, Filomina C.
1994   "The Black Woman Cross-culturally: An Overview." Pp. 7–41 in *The Black Woman Cross-culturally*. Ed. Filomina C. Steady. Rochester, VT: Schenkman.

Schüssler Fiorenza, Elisabeth
1992   *"But She Said": Feminist Practices of Biblical Interpretation*. Boston: Beacon.

Teffo, Joseph
1995   "*Ubuntu/Botho* is how to live." *City Press*, June 25, p. 14.

Waegeman, Maryse
1989   "The Perfect Wife of Proverbia 31:10–31." Pp. 101–7 in *Goldene Äpfel in Silbernen Schalen*. Eds. Klaus-Dietrich Schunck and Matthias Augustin. Frankfurt am Main: Peter Lang.

Washington, Harold C.
1994   "The Strange Woman (אשה זרה/נכריה) of Proverbs 1–9." Pp. 215–42 in *Second Temple Studies. Vol 2: Temple Community in the Persian Period*. Ed. Tamara C. Eskenazi and Kent H. Richards. Sheffield: JSOT.

Whybray, R. N.
1972   *The Book of Proverbs*. Cambridge: Cambridge University Press.

Wolters, Al
1984   "Nature and Grace in the Interpretation of Proverbs 31:10–31." *CTJ* 19: 153–66.

BORDERLESS WOMEN AND BORDERLESS TEXTS: A CULTURAL READING OF MATTHEW 15:21–28

Leticia A. Guardiola-Sáenz
Vanderbilt University

ABSTRACT

As an exercise in cultural studies, this reading focuses not just on the written story and its socio-historical conditions of production, but also on the story as a site where the socio-historical conditions of consumption and the social location of the reader merge with the text to produce a borderless or hybrid "cultural" text. Such a hybrid text is the inception of the story in the cultural space of the reader, where it intermingles with the values, ideologies, and interpretations of the reader who has consumed and experienced the consequences of the interpretation of the story. The Canaanite woman's story is then read through the experience of a Mexican-American reader who crosses the ideological borders of the text to contend that the ideology of chosenness cannot be the final border up to which a reading of this story can go. This alternative reading of the story emerges as the suppressed voice of the Other strives to be heard in the re-casting of the story from the Canaanite woman's point of view. This interpretation comes as a reading strategy of liberation from the imperialistic readings that have been used to oppress and suppress the emergence of the Other.

INTRODUCTION

I am reading Matthew's story with a spirit of dispossession—the one I assume the Canaanite woman had when she approached Jesus: a spirit of protest and reclamation. She was determined to take the bread from the table of those who displaced her, knowing that in a household where even the dogs get to eat what the masters waste, there must be some extra bread for the neighbors—precisely those neighbors whom the masters have dispossessed.

In my socio-historical condition of dispossessed neighbor, born and bred in the borderlands of the U.S. empire, I am certainly determined to take the bread from the table and not wait until the crumbs fall from it. I am convinced that it is only at the level of the table—as equals—and not under the table—as inferiors—that a constructive dialogue and a fair reconstitution of the world can be achieved.

The story of the Canaanite woman has been interpreted and used throughout the centuries to feed and shape the Christian faith in various ways. Although there is a wide variety of interpretations, the vast majority have been performed in complicity with patriarchy and imperialism. For some readers, the male character is seen as playing the leading role—testing the woman's faith—and the woman's role is seen as subordinated to Jesus' role (Garland: 163; Patte: 220). For other readers, the issue of the mission to the Gentiles has blurred the role of the woman (Harrington: 236–38); and for some others, the focus on the presumed priority of one people over others has erased the importance of the woman's identity (France: 247–48; Garland: 165; Levine, 1988:138, 1992:259; Patte: 222). Even those readings which focus on the Canaanite woman as the main character tend to do so in a marginal way. Either they exalt the woman for challenging Jesus' mission, but still depict her as the "humbled dog" (Garland: 165; Patte: 222; Ringe: 68–69; Wainwright, 1994:653); or she is seen as the first fruit of the mission to the Gentiles, the pagan who needs to be redeemed (France: 246; Hare: 178), but not as the Other with a culture and identity of her own and who should be respected for who she is.

In this article I shall present my socially and culturally conditioned interpretation of the Canaanite woman, as a liberating reading strategy, to bring about another fragment of the story that needs to be given voice. I will focus on the Canaanite woman as the Other, the subject with a life that has been silenced and ignored by the dominant structures—a subject who, in the first place, has been victimized by her writer, and in the second place, has been mistreated and incarcerated in the oppressive boundaries of the text or story by her readers.

The writer, on his part, uses her to highlight the priority of one people over others (France: 247–48; Garland: 165; Levine, 1988:138, 1992:259; Patte: 222). With this ideology of chosenness in the background, one cannot expect that the writer will portray the native—the one who has to be dispossessed in order for the chosen one to receive the promised land—as better, or even as equal. Under the totalitarian ideology of chosenness there is no room for the non-elected as Others, but only as the subordinated beings who are used by the chosen ones to define their sameness.

The readers, on their part, have mistreated the Canaanite woman because they continue interpreting her as part of the totality; that is, the social structure in which the oppressed one has been made to believe that he or she has to live under that subordinated condition, and not as Other—one who is different and who deserves to be treated and respected as a different subject. Both the writer and the readers have perpetuated the oppression of the Canaanite woman for their own benefit, maintaining their status quo.

In what follows I shall present first my critical approach to the text, and second my social location. Both will function as the lenses through which I will be re-reading and re-interpreting the story. Finally, I shall conclude with the exposition of my re-construction and re-casting of the story as a liberating reading strategy that is contesting the totalitarian interpretations and giving the Canaanite woman a voice of her own.

CRITICAL APPROACH: CULTURAL STUDIES AND BORDERLESS TEXTS

The boundaries of texts and readers have been defined differently through the years by the different critical approaches. Under the historical-critical paradigm the borders of the texts were clearly defined and limited to the written material through form, redaction, and textual criticisms. In this approach the borders of the reader were universally secured by means of the ideal of the objective perspective. Under literary and cultural criticisms those borders and boundaries began to vanish. Eventually, under cultural studies, the mobility of the readers, their playful irreverence toward the texts, and the cluster of cultures have made all borders blurry.

For cultural studies "a text or practice or event is not the issuing source of meaning, but a site where the articulation of meaning—variable meaning(s)—can take place" (Storey: 4). Every time a text comes in contact with a reader the text becomes a "text": "read and interpreted in a certain way by a certain reader or group of readers at certain time in a certain place" (Segovia, 1995c:325).[1] There are no pure or prototypical texts, with immutable borders, from which we can go and extract the *real* meaning whenever we think that the meaning has been distorted. All interpretations are culturally and biographically mediated. Thus, the existing readings on the Canaanite woman cannot be understood as "objective" or "universal" truths, but as constructions which reflect the social and cultural context of the readers. "The outcome of every interaction, each confrontation between reader and text, is different and unique, temporary and never final" (Rosenau: 26).

A cultural text is not confined to the borders of its written pages, but to the whole culture that embraces its interpretations. To understand its meaning(s) one needs to go beyond and read also the cultural conditions that have surrounded its production and consumption. A cultural text—Matthew's story, in this case—should be read not just for the history it reflects, but also for the history it has made: the political, moral, economic, and social consequences that the text has effected in the culture. As such, a biblical passage is borderless, and can go to infinity and beyond, insofar as many readers read it and transform it into a "text."

In regard to the boundaries and limits of the Bible, the text that has probably exerted more cultural influence on the West than any other single

---

1 For an extended explanation of how Segovia defines cultural studies as a model of interpretation, see Segovia, 1995a and b.

document, the dominant structures have taken special care in keeping them within the hegemonic values. In order for the West to maintain that power of cultural influence, whenever a marginal reading does not conform to those borders or denies them, that reading is considered as biased, not documented in a scholarly manner, or unfaithful to the biblical message and context (Harrington: 238).

Historically, the biblical text has proven to be borderless. The Bible has gone beyond its temporal and spatial boundaries not just for good, but also for the worst destruction. Many people have been erased from the face of the earth and many others have been subjugated and oppressed because they did not conform to the biblically grounded hegemonic ideologies. Thus, after all the massacres done in the name of the Bible, I cannot go to the text with ahistorical and innocent eyes, pretending that the biblical text is harmless.

Following my cultural studies critical approach on borderless texts, I want to contend that, although the ideology of chosenness permeates the Bible, it should not be the only interpretative key nor the biblical text's border limit at which every reading of the Canaanite woman's story should stop. If the ideology of chosenness has proven to be fatal and exploitative to the two-thirds of the world, then it is an ideology that needs to be challenged by all liberative readers. Even if this ideology belongs to the very sacred text that has been used by Western Christianity supposedly to save the Two-Thirds World, it needs to be contested as any other cultural concept or ideology that has been constructed to exploit and subjugate people.

Thus, in my interpretation of the Canaanite woman's story I shall analyze how the Matthean ideology of chosenness is dismantled by the story's plot itself. The very presence of the Canaanite woman, who is used by the author to affirm the chosenness of his people, makes the ideology collapse when she comes, precisely, to confront the one who has advised his disciples to "go nowhere among the Gentiles."

SOCIAL LOCATION: LIVING *SIN FRONTERAS*

I shall begin by telling my own story first, as one considered the other—alien—in this country, one who has been defined and labeled by those who have the power to manipulate history. And second, moving away from that negative position as other, I shall present myself also as the Other: the one who is self-defined, who wants to be treated as different from the totality, and who seeks to engage in a dialogue with the biblical text and its diverse readers—also considered as Others—with whom I shall struggle to make my voice heard and my identity emerge.

As a Mexican-American, with a history of more than two centuries of Spanish colonialism on my back, as well as almost 150 years of neo-colonialism under the United States of America, I cannot help but read the

Canaanite woman's story as a story of protest and reclamation. This is a story of conviction and struggle in which a displaced woman reclaims her place at the table. Reading from my place, I see the dispossessed Canaanite woman demanding the right to be treated as a human being and not as a dog. She acts as if she were convinced that her displacement cannot be the fruit of God's βασιλεία.[2]

In 1848, with the Treaty of Guadalupe-Hidalgo, the ideology of chosenness, the so-called Manifest Destiny, materialized in the United States' expansionism towards Mexico. The unjust appropriation of half of the Mexican territory gave birth to a new reality, the unique world of the Northern Mexican borderlands. Since then, the feelings of displacement and dispossession have been reflected in the continuous crossing of borders by thousands of Mexican-Americans who come to this land to reclaim a slice of life in restitution for the seized territory. No matter how many laws and patrols are enforced to stop the immigration, the influx of boundary-crossers never stops. The hope of reclaiming a better life, and the sense of getting even for the past loss, have promoted the part-time lifestyle in many Mexican-Americans who live half of the year in the U.S. and the other half in Mexico. Those who live this bicultural life learn to be alert to their surroundings, like a chameleon, and to trick the system with the proper skin. Life in the borderlands is a constant metamorphosis and a game of masks. Smuggling has become the ethos of survival. What is at stake is not just the material smuggling of goods, but also the lives of those who are at risk every time they cross the borderlands. According to Gloria Anzaldúa, in order "to survive the Borderlands you must live *sin fronteras*, be a crossroads" (402).

Read through my experience, the story of the Canaanite woman is the encounter of two peoples, two cultures in contest. It is a story of borderland conflicts between the original inhabitants and those who have dispossessed them, with a long history of struggle, rupture, and hybridity. But it is also a romantic view of the other, the submissive image depicted by the Totality, which needs to be unmasked and retold from the solid ground of a postcolonial world. A text that conceals the ideology of a manifest destiny and a chosenness of people, which allows the displacement of Others from their own land and does not condemn such ideology as oppressive, cannot be a liberating text when it is interpreted by those in power, who want to keep the power for themselves. It is only by listening to the voice of the Other in the text, the one who has suffered the unjust invasion and oppression, that one can construct a liberating story. In order to bring justice to the story of

---

2 Although I consider the concept of βασιλεία as God's ultimate blessing for humanity, I criticize the Matthean construction of it. Matthew, as a writer from a people that has emerged and grown as a nation with an ideology of chosenness, a common ideology among the imperialistic nations, reduces the concept of βασιλεία by filtering it through that oppressive ideology.

the woman, I intend to construct the story from the point of view of the native of the land.

As such, my reading is an act of self-affirmation and solidarity with the Canaanite woman as Other. It is an effort to construct, not just my own Otherness through the re-interpretation of the story, but also the Otherness of the Canaanite woman, by defying the harmful borders of the biblical text. This will be part of my liberating reading strategy against the imperialistic practices. It is a step forward in the process of decolonization and liberation, a process that cultural studies has brought into biblical criticism by means of the contextualized flesh-and-blood reader. My reading as a real reader of the Canaanite woman's story is an act of re-appropriation of the text, a move to re-write the story from the reverse of history. My reading is a story re-told by the defeated, re-written from the inter-space of the post-colonial reader. This re-casting of the story is also a way of speaking from the borderless biblical text that has been inscribed in culture for centuries. From this angle I now question: What if the Canaanite woman was aware of her dispossession? What if she was not begging Jesus for a favor but demanding restitution? What if she was not worshiping Jesus but defying him? What if I really recast the story? Would that attempt change the history of exploitation and destruction that the ideology of chosenness has endorsed? In what follows, I will therefore be revisiting the text from my own space and experience, knowing that the conventions of writing did not give the woman the chance to speak by herself; and that even if it is a constructed story, it does not eliminate the possibility that there was first an event that could have been misread by the author in his insistence on a totalitarian voice.

RE-CASTING THE STORY: WHAT IF . . . ? ·

By comparing the story of the Canaanite woman in Matthew's Gospel with the narrative of the Syro-Phoenician woman in Mark's Gospel, I can notice that the stories respond to different contexts and different purposes. The first evident difference between them is the geographic location of Jesus in the story. While in Mark we read that Jesus is the one crossing the borderlands of Tyre and Sidon, in Matthew we read that Jesus remains in his territory.[3] The established pattern of the mission given to the disciples by Jesus in Matt 10:5–6 ("Go nowhere among the Gentiles") helps us to locate Jesus out of Tyre and Sidon. This leads us to read in 15:22 that the Canaanite woman is the one crossing the borderlands.

---

[3] In Matthew's story the issue of Jesus crossing the border could be debatable, but where we locate Jesus depends on how we translate the preposition εἰς—whether as "into" or as "to," "towards." To be consistent with the Matthean vision of Jesus' earthly mission I will adopt the meaning "to." See Levine, 1988:137; and Harrington: 235.

According to Amy-Jill Levine, the fact that the woman meets Jesus in his own territory implies that she is accepting the temporal priority of the Jews, a priority that is reinforced in Matthew when the woman is called a Canaanite, and when she calls Jesus "son of David" (Levine, 1988:138). The woman's identity and the title she uses for Jesus link the story to the Jewish ancient history—the fight against the original inhabitants to possess the land of Canaan and the ancient monarchy of Israel. For Levine, once more, this means that "just as the Jews had priority over the Canaanites in the past, so too they retain this priority in the present" (Levine, 1988:138). This priority is also invoked in the parallel story of the Syro-Phoenician woman, who, according to Elisabeth Schüssler Fiorenza, "respects the primacy of the 'children of Israel'" (97).

Reading Levine's statement in light of what Matthew presents as Jesus' mission to the Gentiles, I do believe that her logic of interpretation is quite close to the logic that is reflected in the rhetoric of Matthew's Gospel. Matthew frames the woman as a weak and humble person who comes to see Jesus—the one whom the story presents as having power, regardless of the historical and political situation of the people of Israel in this historical moment. She is depicted as requesting Jesus' mercy, and calling him "Lord, son of David," as a sign that she is accepting his preeminence. In Matthew's view, the Canaanite woman is the subordinated being that recognizes the priority of the Chosen People—those who have defined themselves as the dominant Totality, the autocracy of the house of Israel that permeates the whole text, and an ideology that remains present even in times of their Roman oppression, as in this story. The woman is denied her identity as Other. If her capacity as dialectic opponent is erased, then she has no power to break the oppressive uni-dimensionalism of the Totality in which she has been constrained by the author.[4]

In my opinion, Matthew's logic of the story is the same sort of monolithic logic that is incapable of perceiving and accepting the Other as different. Therefore, to find a liberating reading of the Canaanite woman's story, it is imperative to realize that Matthew's "romantic presentation of the other as a liminal figure hinders a recognition of the social and historical specificity of the Other as the oppressed and derogated figures within a dominant system" (McNay: 80).

In my re-casting of the story, Matthew's attempt to portray the Canaanite woman as the romantic other who is used to define the sameness of the chosen ones makes him lose sight of the woman as the dialectic Other, the one who opposes by definition the oppressive system. It is at this angle of the story where I want to ground my reading, precisely where Matthew has

---

4 For the relationship between oppressor and oppressed, which constitutes the Totality that hinders the emergence of the Other as such, see Dussel: 11–33.

failed to recognize the "social and historical specificity of the Other" (McNay: 80). It is as if the character escapes from his hands in search of a new author who can understand and respect her identity as the socially and culturally Other that she is. The latent Otherness of the Canaanite woman, overlooked and suppressed by Matthew, is now growing louder and awakening the post-colonial readers with her cry for liberation from the totalitarian system that has abducted her.

If we go back now to v. 22, with the awareness of the Other and of her cultural and historical background, the fact that the Canaanite woman crosses the border gains a new meaning. Consequently, I can read the story with a different tone, or I should say I can listen to a different tone in the woman's voice. This voice rises with a tone of anger of the displaced and rebellious woman in search of her Otherness. It is no longer the tone of the submissive whisper of the alienated. In listening to this tone of protest, I want to contend that she crosses the border not to worship the dispossessor, but subtly to demand restitution. She is fighting back against the oppressor by disrupting and invading the geographical space from which she has been displaced. She is coming to get compensation for what was taken away from her. Her cry for mercy before the son of David is a cry of restitution. I can hear that she knows the proper formula and tone for such a plea. By using the language of the system, "son of David" as a confession of faith, she ironically flatters the one in power in order to get away with her smuggling and sneaking business in the contested borderlands. Therefore, the woman's action of crossing the borders and confronting the one in power—the son of David—leads me to construct the Other, from the very beginning, as a strong and determined individual, which is the opposite of the submissive woman that the writer, and his ideology of chosenness, wants to portray.

Furthermore, the recognition of Jesus as the son of David is not a statement of faith on the lips of the Canaanite woman. It is an asseveration of protest and a demand that she who has been dispossessed raises to disrupt the comfort of the invader. By calling the oppressor by his status of power, and by standing in front of him, the woman asserts with her presence that her condition as oppressed is the consequence of his privileges. Confronting the oppressive system with its atrocities, and doing so by its own language, is at once a survival strategy of the Other and a direct result of her presence and her very identity as oppressed. She will not rest until the oppressor realizes that the cost of his privileges is not just the dehumanization of the oppressed, but his own dehumanization. That effect on himself is due to his inability to respect and engage in dialogue with the Other.

If we read the text within the broader scenarios of Matthew's Gospel we can notice that the Canaanite woman's story has been framed by the writer in the midst of the abundance and prosperity of the βασιλεία. By placing the story of the dispossessed in the middle of the richness of the invader's empire—framed by stories of abundance of bread (14:13–21; 15:30–38) and health (9:27–31; 20:29–34)—the author contrasts and justifies the prosperity of the ancient invaders as a divine blessing. At the same time, the author contrasts the poverty of the Canaanites as God's curse for their presence in what was God's promised land for the chosen ones.

Following the rhetoric of the Other who defies Matthew's rhetoric, I see the story of the Canaanite woman in the vertex of a chiastic structure—dispossession and oppression being revealed as the empire's rotation axis. The good news about Jesus' miraculous deeds and the stories about inexhaustible food get the interest of the Canaanite woman, who comes to witness such abundance and to request her indemnity. The hour of the dispossessed has come. In the midst of the wasteland, the Canaanite woman defies, with her presence and her demand, Matthew's construction of the βασιλεία.

Such courage and determination on the part of the Other, who has awakened to the injustice of the system and comes to claim respect and restitution, leaves Jesus speechless (15:23). What Matthew creates as a strident silence of indifference—the oppressor's response to the pain of the oppressed—is transformed by the dialectic presence of the Other into a silence of astonishment. The image of the wicked Canaanites, who supposedly offer their children in sacrifice to their gods (Segal: 19), is challenged by this fearless Canaanite woman who comes to smuggle out life for her daughter from the dispossessor, putting her own life at risk in the venture. In this way, the mock evil image of the Other, fabricated and used by the empire as an instrument of oppression, is shaken and demolished by the very presence and request of the Canaanite woman. She is articulating her humanity. The borderless Other confronts the Totality by revealing her otherness, which, ironically and to the distress of the empire, resembles the otherness of those who dominate within the Totality.

The disciples, frightened by the cry of justice raised by the rebellious woman, awaken Jesus from his absorption by begging for help. Whenever the subversive oppressed emerge, the oppressor tends to give a quick reply, more from fear of a revolt than from human compassion. I see this fearful response in the disciples, who want her far away quickly, and who are willing to give up some of their privileges (15:23). Compelled by his disciples, the Jesus of Matthew, who is clearly aware of the chosenness of his people and their privileges, re-asserts the exclusiveness of his mission (10:5; 15:24).

The writer, in an effort to stop and prevent the rise of the Other as such, pretends to camouflage in v. 25 the Canaanite woman's act of bravery and challenge as an act of humiliation and submissive worshiping of the dominant Totality. By trying to depict the Other in a diminished position and promoting such a position as desirable, the oppressor seeks to alienate the oppressed woman and hinder her from being conscious of her oppression, and therefore from rejecting it.

In contrast, on the other side of the border, this response of exclusivism that Jesus gives to his disciples, while ignoring the Canaanite woman—a response that evokes the imperialistic tendencies of the Monroe Doctrine—is openly ignored by the woman when she confronts them. Seeing them in uncertainty—the disciples urging Jesus to act, and Jesus trying to convince them and probably himself that that was not the right thing to do—the woman approaches Jesus to make her petition clear and sound. She breaks their dialogue, and she breaks the borders of their communication to make her voice heard. As an act of complete openness, the woman kneels before Jesus, challenging with the vulnerability of her otherness Jesus' own otherness. A woman without boundaries—*sin fronteras*—becomes a boundary for Jesus. With her own body she blocks Jesus' way, putting herself as a boundary which Jesus should respect, a boundary that was not respected when the Israelites conquered the land.

In his last attempt to resist the Canaanite woman, who is defying the order of the system by establishing boundaries for the boundary-less, the Chosen's strategy of intimidation emerges as a violent insult. The writer makes the oppressor use offensive words to remind the oppressed that she is less than the oppressor. Gerd Theissen says that "Jesus' rejection of the woman expresses a bitterness that had built up within the relationships between Jews and Gentiles in the border regions between Tyre and Galilee" (65). But it is a bitterness that the woman, convinced of what she wants and of who she is, rejects with honor and respect. Her response reminds the oppressors that their wealth, unless they share it with their neighbors to compensate what they have taken, will continue to dehumanize them. The woman asserts that if the dogs, which are animals, get to eat what their masters waste, she, who is the Other, can break the bread together with the masters. Contrary to the opinions of most interpreters, I argue that the Canaanite woman does not identify herself as a dog. When she says "Yes, Lord," she is agreeing with Jesus that it would be absurd to throw away the children's bread to the dogs. But at the same time she reminds him that if even their dogs are eating from what their masters waste (which implies plenty), with more reason she is entitled to bread.

She demands to be considered as Other, and breaks into the empire. She cannot and does not respect either human boundaries or divine boundaries that go against the human value of life. She breaks the boundaries of ethnicity, of the empire, of gender, of culture, and speaks for her daughter: she speaks for the one who cannot speak, for the one who cannot move, for the one who has no strength to fight back against the empire of the male oppressor and against God as male. She presents to Jesus the wide world outside of the empire, the need of those who are oppressed by the empire. The Canaanite woman reclaims respectful treatment as Other under what she supposes is the new reign of equality: the βασιλεία, which has come to break the empires. Confronted with such a declaration of confidence and self-affirmation, witnessing the emergence of the Canaanite woman as his dialectic Other, Jesus can do no other than respond positively to the woman's request. Jesus understands her demand and moves back from what he thought was his mission to give the woman the place that she deserves at the table.

This conclusion is warranted by the question why, if Jesus himself said to his disciples "go nowhere among the Gentiles," he did not reject her firmly, but instead chose to help her? Clearly it is because the totalitarian people were not ready to receive the stranger. They expelled the Canaanites from their land, but they were not planning to go out of their way to help them. They did not think that the Other would come to confront them. "Go nowhere among the Gentiles" is a good command, but what does one do when the oppressed come? What happens when the Other refuses to be treated as other or oppressed, when the Canaanite woman refuses to conform to the role that the totality wants her to play? What happens when the invaded and dispossessed becomes the invader and the dispossessor? The woman's presence is already a way of showing the resistance of the oppressed people, holding that the present system of oppression does not have to remain in place. Her presence is already the evidence that the dispossessed woman is fighting back on her own terms, with her own arms. She is not waiting for justice. She is taking justice in her hands, in the same way as do the Mexican workers who cross the border and come to the U.S., which, as some point out, dispossessed them from their territory.

As Mexicans, we know that the U.S. will not help us get our land back. Therefore, the only way of getting back something of what they took from us is by re-invading the land. It is by coming north to work without asking immigration to give us legal papers. It is by striving to have a better life even if the price is hiding and running from the system. As Gloria Anzaldúa says, to survive in the Borderlands we have to live *sin fronteras*.

To conclude, as a Mexican-American I have read the Canaanite woman's story with the rhetoric of the Other against the rhetoric of Matthew and its readers. I hold that the Canaanite woman is not a humble dog begging for crumbs. She is a dispossessed woman who has awoken from her position as oppressed, and now is coming to confront the empire and demand her right to be treated as human. By asking Jesus to heal her daughter, the Canaanite woman is asking for a restitution that will not just vindicate her as Other, but will also vindicate her oppressor as Other. The presence of the woman as the resistant oppressed, who has gained consciousness of her oppression, is finally breaking the Totalitarian system. She is confronting the oppressor. He, in turn, realizes on account of her presence as Other that he has overridden her rights and ignored her existence, but now he has been humanized by her presence. The Other that he once treated as a dog is now giving him a lesson of human courage and love for life. The Canaanite woman has come to break the bread together with him as an act of restitution and humanization.

WORKS CONSULTED

Anzaldúa, Gloria
1994   "To Live in the Borderlands Means You . . ." Pp. 401–2 in *Barrios and Borderlands: Cultures of Latinos and Latinas in the United States*. Ed. Denis Lynn Daly Heyck. New York: Routledge.

Dussel, Enrique
1987   *Liberación de la Mujer y Erótica Latinoamericana: Ensayo Filosófico*. Tercera Edición. Bogotá: Nueva América.

France, R. T.
1985   *The Gospel According to Matthew*. Grand Rapids: Eerdmans.

Garland, David E.
1993   *Reading Matthew*. New York: Crossroad.

Golub, Jacob S.
1930   *Israel in Canaan*. Cincinnati: Department of Synagogue and School Extension of the Union of American Hebrew Congregations.

Hare, Douglas R. A.
1993   *Matthew. Interpretation: A Bible Commentary for Teaching and Preaching*. Louisville: John Knox.

Harrington, Daniel J.
1991   *The Gospel of Matthew*. Sacra Pagina Series 1. Collegeville: Liturgical.

Kwok, Pui-lan
1995   *Discovering the Bible in the Non-Biblical World*. Maryknoll: Orbis.

Levine, Amy-Jill
1988   *The Social and Ethnic Dimensions of Matthean Salvation History*. Lewiston: Edwin Mellen.

1992   "Matthew." Pp. 252–62 in *The Women's Bible Commentary*. Ed. Carol A. Newsom and Sharon H. Ringe. Louisville: Westminster/John Knox.

Luz, Ulrich
1994   *Matthew in History*. Minneapolis: Fortress.

McNay, Lois
1994   *Foucault: A Critical Introduction*. New York: Continuum.

Patte, Daniel
1987   *The Gospel according to Matthew: A Structural Commentary on Matthew's Faith*. Philadelphia: Fortress.

Ringe, Sharon H.
1985   "A Gentile Woman's Story." Pp. 65–72 in *Feminist Interpretation of the Bible*. Ed. Letty M. Russell. Philadelphia: Westminster.

Rosenau, Pauline Marie
1992   *Post-modernism and the Social Sciences: Insights, Inroads, and Intrusions.* Princeton: Princeton University Press.

Schüssler Fiorenza, Elisabeth
1992   *But She Said: Feminist Practices of Biblical Interpretation.* Boston: Beacon.

Segal, Alan F.
1986   *Rebecca's Children.* Cambridge: Harvard University Press.

Segovia, Fernando F.
1995a   "'And They Began to Speak in Other Tongues': Competing Modes of Discourse in Contemporary Biblical Criticism." Pp. 1–32 in *Reading from This Place. Vol. 1: Social Location and Biblical Interpretation in the United States.* Ed. Fernando F. Segovia and Mary Ann Tolbert. Minneapolis: Fortress.

1995b   "Toward a Hermeneutics of the Diaspora: A Hermeneutics of Otherness and Engagement." Pp. 57–73 in *Reading from this Place. Vol. 1: Social Location and Biblical Interpretation in the United States.* Ed. Fernando F. Segovia and Mary Ann Tolbert. Minneapolis: Fortress.

1995c   "Toward Intercultural Criticism: A Reading Strategy from the Diaspora." Pp. 303–30 in *Reading from This Place. Vol. 2: Social Location and Biblical Interpretation in Global Perspective.* Ed. Fernando F. Segovia and Mary Ann Tolbert. Minneapolis: Fortress.

Storey, John
1996   *Cultural Studies and the Study of Popular Culture: Theories and Methods.* Athens: University of Georgia Press.

Theissen, Gerd
1991   *The Gospels in Context: Social and Political History in the Synoptic Tradition.* Trans. Linda M. Maloney. Minneapolis: Fortress.

Wainwright, Elaine M.
1994   "The Gospel of Matthew." Pp. 635–77 in *Searching the Scriptures. Vol. 2. A Feminist Commentary.* Ed. Elisabeth Schüssler Fiorenza. New York: Crossroad.

1995   "A Voice from the Margin: Reading Matthew 15:21–28 in an Australian Feminist Key." Pp. 132–53 in *Reading from This Place. Vol 2: Social Location and Biblical Interpretation in Global Perspective.* Ed. Fernando F. Segovia and Mary Ann Tolbert. Minneapolis: Fortress.

Warrior, Robert Allen
1991   "A Native American Perspective: Canaanites, Cowboys, and Indians." Pp. 287–95 in *Voices from the Margin.* Ed. R. S. Sugirtharajah. Maryknoll: Orbis.

Young, Robert J. C.
1995   *Colonial Desire: Hybridity in Theory, Culture and Race.* London: Routledge.

READING THE BIBLE "WITH" WOMEN IN POOR AND MARGINALIZED COMMUNITIES IN SOUTH AFRICA[1]

Malika Sibeko and Beverley Haddad
University of Natal

ABSTRACT

Liberation theologians have long argued that the key question in theology and biblical studies is who one's dialogue partners are in the doing of theology and in the reading of the Bible. In other words, who are our primary interlocutors? This essay takes this question seriously, choosing to place "ordinary" (academically untrained) women readers of the Bible at the center. Women readers of the Bible, particularly when they are ordinary, poor, African women readers, are usually marginalized and subjugated readers of the Bible. This essay explores the reading processes and products that take place when such women are given the opportunity to speak. Mark 5:21–6:1 is the focal text for the study.

Reading the Bible "with" women in poor and marginalized communities in South Africa poses particular challenges, given their context of cultural, economic, and ecclesiastical oppression. This paper reflects the corporate work of the Institute for the Study of the Bible, which uses a methodology that emphasizes reading the Bible "with" rather than "for" these communities, and illustrates a reading of Mark 5:21–6:1 by women of Amawoti, an informal settlement in KwaZulu-Natal, South Africa.

South Africa has a population of forty million, of which about fifty percent are women. Poverty is one of the great burdens of the country. According to the African National Congress, there are at least seventeen million people surviving below the "Minimum Living Level" (14). Wilson and Ramphele assert (190–201) that the causes of this poverty can be traced back to the periods of conquest of the sixteenth and seventeenth centuries, and to nineteenth-century colonialism in South African history. Out of the colonial period of slavery (ended by the British in 1834), the capitalist economy emerged. True emancipation did not follow the abolition of slavery. In its place, an intricate system of "pass laws" and vagrancy laws developed, which became the foundation of the migratory labor system. This system has been fundamental in meeting the needs of an exploitative modern capi-

---

1 An earlier version of this paper can be found in the *Bulletin for Contextual Theology in Southern Africa and Africa* 3:1996.

talist society. In the next phase (the early twentieth century), a systematic assault on the industrial labor movement prevented any significant advancement of the black population (Wilson and Ramphele: 192) From this period the beginnings of the vast discrepancy between rich and poor and between black and white emerged in modern South Africa—a discrepancy that was consolidated with the coming to power of the National Party in 1948. The grand scheme of apartheid was put into operation during the 1950s and 1960s, ultimately affecting every area of social life for the vast majority of the population. The system of apartheid guaranteed that political, economic, and cultural power was controlled by the white minority. Social deprivation was heightened even further by the policy of separate development resulting in the forced removal of millions of people from their homes and a restrictive urbanization policy directed towards African people, implemented through pass laws and influx control measures. With the lifting of these influx controls and the replacement of the pass document with a uniform identity document for all race groups in 1986, the rate of urbanization increased significantly. This rapid urbanization process coupled with a huge backlog in the provision of housing, has resulted in massive overcrowding in the urban townships and the development of large-scale peri-urban informal settlements.

The community of Amawoti situated in KwaZulu-Natal is one of these settlements with an estimated population of one hundred thousand (Philpott: 32) It falls just outside the official boundaries of Durban, one of the fastest growing cities in the world. Few basic services are available to the community. Housing is constructed from wattle and mud, corrugated iron and packing cases. Until recently there was no piped water, sewerage system, electricity, or adequate rubbish removal. Education and health facilities are minimal. It is estimated that fifty-one per cent of economically active people are unemployed (Philpott: 33). Furthermore, because of its situation in a politically volatile region, Amawoti has been the subject of ongoing violence between different political groupings. Economically it is also fractured, with landowners of the area renting out land to others. Despite these hardships, Amawoti is a community full of life and vibrancy and has been described as a "place of suffering and hope" (Philpott: 28).

And what of women?

African women in South Africa have experienced what many womanists and feminists call the "triple oppression" of race, class, and gender. It is only recently that it has been acknowledged that the majority of the poor are women. *The Reconstruction and Development Programme: A Policy Framework* (African National Congress) is the first official document in South Africa to acknowledge the subordinated status of women and make recommendations to redress their legal, economic, and political status. However, even this document fails adequately to involve women in the analysis and restructuring of patriarchal society (Agenda Collective).

The subordination of women is even more evident in the church, even though they are in the majority in most congregations. While many of the missionary-initiated churches now ordain women to positions of ministerial leadership, the numbers coming forward for ordination are comparatively few. Church structures continue to be patriarchal and male-dominated. In the African Independent Churches (to which the majority of the women of Amawoti in the Bible study process belong) the situation is no different. Women are excluded from performing baptisms and distributing Holy Communion, and there is a pervasive attitude arising from a complex interplay of cultural practice and the Levitical texts that women are "unclean" as a result of menstruation. Those that are in lay leadership are prevented from performing duties when they are menstruating. And so the church too remains a site of struggle.

Throughout the above social and ecclesiastical history, the Bible has played and will continue to play a significant role in the life of Christians in South Africa. During the late 1980s, political violence ravaged KwaZulu-Natal, with people dying daily. Communities directly affected were asking, "What is God saying to us in this situation?" Trained biblical scholars and those reading the Bible in these communities met in an attempt to discover together what God was saying in this context of suffering. Out of this collaboration, the Institute for the Study of the Bible (ISB) was founded in 1990. It is linked to the School of Theology at the University of Natal, Pietermaritzburg, and to a number of church and community organizations. "The primary aim of the ISB is to establish an interface between biblical studies and ordinary readers of the Bible in the church and the community that will facilitate social transformation" (West, 1993:76).

Crucial to the reading of Mark 5:21–6:1 with women of Amawoti is the methodology used by ISB. This reading methodology involves four commitments.[2] The first is a commitment to read the Bible from the perspective of organized communities of the poor and oppressed in the South African context. It is essentially a commitment to begin with the perceived reality of the poor and oppressed, defined by West as "those who are socially, politically, economically, or culturally marginalized and exploited" (1993:13). Hence the reading of this text by women of Amawoti will be explicitly shaped by their particular reality of oppression in their churches, their community, and within the wider South African society. The second commitment is to read the Bible in community. This is a recognition that the contributions of both trained and ordinary readers are different, but equally significant. In recognizing the subjectivity of both groups, all the readers become active participants, and not just the biblical scholar. Facilitators from the ISB thus read the text "with" women of Amawoti rather than "to" or "for" them. The third

---

2 For fuller discussion see West, 1993:12–22.

commitment is to critical modes of reading the Bible. This commitment stresses the importance of developing a "critical consciousness" by readers, which questions the status quo and uses a systematic and structured analysis of text and society. Bible reading, and the Bible itself, are not devoid of ideology that results in political, cultural, economic, and gender bias. These biases need to be unmasked in order to ensure that the hermeneutical process is liberatory and not oppressive. Sharing critical resources with ordinary readers to facilitate this unmasking is a particular contribution trained readers can offer to the process. The fourth and final commitment is to personal and social transformation through the contextual Bible study process. This transformation includes "the existential, the political, the economic, the cultural, and the religious spheres of life" (West, 1993:21). In order for this to occur, West points out, there needs to be an ongoing dialogue between the text and its context on the one hand, and the participants and their context on the other (1993:67). This presupposes that a critical appropriation of the Mark text by women of Amawoti will be a process that needs an ongoing dialogue among themselves around the text in relation to their particular relations and social context.

A reading of the Mark text was first conducted by the ISB with a group of women in Umtata, a rural town in South Africa (West, 1995). Facilitating the Bible study process in Amawoti, as in Umtata, involved no prior exegesis of the text, and only three questions were asked for discussion in the group:

1. Read Mark 5:21–6:1 and discuss what the text is about.
2. Can we say this text is about women and why?
3. How does this text apply to you as women in your context?

The first question was used to encourage the participants to read the text carefully and closely. The second question invited participants to look at the text once more, but also provided an opportunity to raise questions about the society that produced the text. Finally, the text and the context of the readers are drawn together in an act of appropriation (West, 1995).

When invited to respond to the first question, the following themes emerged: healing, power, hope, faith, and trust. Salvation was particularly emphasized because the vernacular translation used by the readers translated "healing" as "salvation." Responding to the second question, the readers felt that the text was about women. When asked to substantiate this response, the following reasons were given:

• The two main characters that Jesus dealt with were Jairus' daughter and the woman who was bleeding.
• Both of these women were in trouble and in need.

- Both had faith and trust that they would be healed.
- They were true believers.

The women of Amawoti immediately identified with the woman with the hemorrhage in the text. Discussion followed concerning this woman's situation. The readers pointed out that even Jairus' daughter was known in relationship to someone. However, the woman with the hemorrhage had no name, no relationship, and was known only by her illness (v. 25). Her situation defined both her name and her personhood. There was speculation as to what might have happened if the woman had not revealed herself to Jesus (v. 33). The readers felt that Jesus had made it possible by his attitude. He had not regarded the woman as unclean and had affirmed her by healing her (v. 29). It was also acknowledged, however, that the woman herself had shown courage and inner strength by taking the initiative. In spite of her circumstances, there was a recognition that she had never given up hope through-out the twelve years. Through the encounter the woman was given "the right to talk to Jesus."

The reason why power left Jesus after the healing (v. 30) became a key concern of the readers. They wrestled together to try to understand what this meant. A debate ensued as to whether this loss of power was a result of his having "touched a bleeding woman," or whether it was necessary for the power to leave Jesus ("be revealed") in order for the woman "to be made holy." In other words, did the power leave Jesus because as a holy teacher he had been contaminated by an unclean woman, or was the power given by Jesus to the woman in order for healing and wholeness to occur? No conclusions were reached, but there were indications of a stronger voice for the latter opinion.

When the final question was asked on how the text applied to their situation as women, issues arose that related primarily to church practice. Once again the issue of Jesus' loss of power was raised. The male leaders of the African Independent Church to which the readers belonged insist that they cannot lay hands on a women when she is menstruating, as this will result "in the loss of their power." As members of this church, a high priority is placed on the laying on of hands, together with prayer, for healing from emotional, spiritual, or physical illness. One reader referred to feeling depressed while menstruating when she met other women who were able to receive the laying on of hands. She then felt "like a sick person." The women began to voice their anger at the fact that they were being denied crucial spiritual resources (laying on of hands, prayer, healing) by the male leadership who were "forcing power away from them." Their personhood was being defined by their state of "bleeding," so their "bleeding" was more important to the church leadership than their spiritual, emotional, or physical needs.

A further issue raised pertained to the practice of women not being allowed to wear church uniforms during menstruation, and thus being forced to sit at the entrance to the worship area. One woman suggested that because this was the case, they should not bother to go to church and "just stay home." Another reflected that it did not make sense for her not to put her uniform on when "her body is the temple of God." As the temple of God, she should not be obliged to participate in the customary purification rite that takes place after seven days. This same reader indignantly noted that the purification ceremony sprinkled holy water on her uniform that she had not worn during menstruation, on the church building she had not entered, and on the congregation with whom she had not associated. If the ceremony was important for "purification," why was she who was regarded as unclean not sprinkled with water? This led to a recognition by others that perhaps they had a choice after all. They had the choice either to stay at home or to put on their uniform and go to church!

Furthermore, the readers pointed out that the practice of separation of women from men during menstruation was a cultural practice that had arisen when families lived in large communal complexes. Within the family complex there would have been a separate hut for "unclean women." Now due to current social and economic circumstances, families lived in a two or three room dwelling. Men and women were thus forced during menstruation to sleep in the same bed, eat from the same dishes, and wash in the same buckets. The bishop was therefore being inconsistent by retaining a cultural practice that was inappropriate to current social and economic circumstances. He received food from an "unclean" wife and then went on to serve Holy Communion. It was suggested (amidst much laughter) that "the bishop should cook his own food and not sleep in the same bed as his wife" before coming to church during this time of the month, or else he too was "unclean." The fact that women in leadership positions were obliged to relinquish their duties to others during menstruation made no sense when the congregation was being served by an "unclean" bishop. Church practice has been influenced by cultural practice with the help of the Levitical texts, though just what the relationship is between culture and text in this case requires further research. In any event, this form of discrimination against women "should diminish, as it no longer suits our situation at this time."

Finally, issues concerning faith were raised by the reading of the text. The women of Amawoti had been deeply challenged by the faith of the bleeding woman. They recognized that until then their oppressive situation had had a debilitating effect on their lives and had led to a loss of faith. In the text they identified a call to "have faith" and felt "strengthened in faith" through the discovery of the woman with no name who never lost hope throughout the twelve long years. This was an encouragement to never lose hope in spite of their social and ecclesiastical circumstances, which might then lead to a change of heart among the male leadership. It they had courage to draw near to Jesus "as a man," as the woman in the story had done, there would be rewards for this trust and faith. "This text tells us as women to trust, believe, pray, and never stop. It tells us not to be shy as women in this new South Africa. We need to stand up as equal partners with men and enjoy our rights."

The reading that has been outlined offers a number of significant insights about reading the Bible "with" ordinary women in South Africa. While reading Mark 5:21–6:1 as a literary unit enables readers to read this text as a text about women, the Amawoti women readers focused on only one woman's story. The contextual Bible study process in its commitment to begin with the perceived reality of the ordinary marginalized reader allows the reading to take this shape. Amawoti women identified so strongly with the bleeding woman that the healing of Jairus' daughter became incidental. Their perceived reality of oppression as a result of menstruation shaped the entire reading of the text.

By allowing the readers' perceived reality to shape the reading of the text, the trained readers were acknowledging their subjectivity in the process. This acknowledgment facilitated mutual learning. Reading the text "with" the women of Amawoti rather than "for" them highlighted the significance of menstruation as a tool of oppression for this community. The facilitators then began to question whether this was true for all African communities. Reading the text communally has thus uncovered new insights, which have become the stimulus for further research.

Work mentioned earlier with the women of Umtata (West, 1995) seemed to suggest that while menstruation had been an issue, it had not held the same significance in their reading. This was a racialy mixed group comprised of English and Xhosa speaking women. Therefore, the question arises whether menstruation was particularly important among the Amawoti women because they were Zulu speaking. Was it central to their reading because they were all African women? Was it important to them as members of an African Independent Church that institutionalizes oppressive church practice? Had the fact that the facilitators were female played a role? These questions have encouraged the facilitators to read this text with additional groups of African women.

To date, one reading of the same text has been carried out with a large gathering of Zulu speaking Methodist women in Sobantu, an established township in Pietermaritzburg. Using the same Bible study methodology and text, a similar reading to that of the women of Amawoti emerged. This reading too was shaped entirely by the issue of menstruation. For the purposes of this article, the reading by the women of Sobantu will not be fully outlined. Suffice it to say that of particular note were the differences that existed within this group of women over the menstruation issue. The Sobantu women as Methodists are not confronted with the same oppressive institutional church practice on the menstruation issue as the Amawoti women. Yet some of these women of their own volition choose not to take Holy Communion when they are menstruating. Some Sobantu readers were of the opinion that they did experience "less power during this time of the month." When this view was expressed, other readers challenged them strongly "to sort themselves out." A specific dynamic in this reading process was the fact that one of the facilitators was an African ordained minister in the Methodist church. This seemed to provide the safe space for the women to discuss their differences. They vigorously questioned the facilitator about matters that had not been made explicit in Amawoti. Did she feel comfortable distributing Holy Communion when she was menstruating? Did she preach during this time? If so, did she feel she had "less power"? She unabashedly confessed that during menstruation she "had even more power"!

Other hermeneutical observations on the reading of Mark 5:21–6:1 by the Amawoti women should be noted. The readers experienced difficulty reading the text closely and carefully, which resulted in sparse responses to the first two questions. Their understanding of the text emerged more fully when asked to apply the text to their context. How these ordinary readers use the Bible in their daily life of faith thus became clear in their appropriation of the text. This same observation is made by Draper and West (40), who state that ordinary readers "believe, hope, and act" with little or no "expert" biblical knowledge. Of further interest is the way the Amawoti readers understood the social situation of the woman with the hemorrhage. As already mentioned, they noted that she was in relationship to no one. Other readings carried out by the ISB (West, 1995) have indicated that Jairus' daughter was oppressed because she was defined in patriarchal terms through the relationship with her father. However, for the Amawoti readers this daughter at least had a relationship with someone, whereas the bleeding woman had no relationship. This was a far greater sorrow.

The question of Jesus' power played a central role in the discussion. In trying to discern what actually was meant by "the power had gone forth from him" (v. 30), the women were focusing on a crucial hermeneutical issue in their lives. The male leadership of the church cites this verse as the basis for using their institutional power to disempower those under their authority. They argue that because power left Jesus when he was touched by a bleeding woman, they too would lose power in their ministry if they touched menstruating women. But for the women readers, Jesus intended to use his power to empower the disempowered. Through the Bible study process the readers began to question the interpretive distortion by the church leadership.

The Amawoti women also began to appropriate the faith of the woman in the text in a particular way through their perceived reality of oppression as a result of menstruation. For them the faith of this woman took on significant proportions. Her faith enabled her to reach wholeness and to be defined in a new way. Her personhood was now defined, not by illness, but by wholeness. In the process of reading the text their faith was strengthened and a vision of wholeness nurtured. The reading of Mark 5:21–6:1 by these ordinary South African women of faith thus highlights the dynamic forces that operate when reader and text are brought together. The faith of the bleeding woman becomes the source of faith for these women in their daily lives of cultural, economic, and ecclesiastical oppression.

As facilitators it would be arrogant to suggest that these women readers have been definitively transformed and empowered through this particular Bible study. There are, however, tentative indications that a process of empowerment has begun from their reading of this text. Meeting together as women, to study a text facilitated by women, enabled the readers (and the facilitators) to explore the oppressive effects of menstruation on their lives, perhaps for the first time publicly in a group. The contextual Bible study process as a process became liberatory as it enabled women to speak unspoken words. This liberating experience led to a request for further Bible studies, as the readers yearned for more unspoken possibilities. Empowerment had thus resulted through both the process and the product of the reading.

The effects of the reading did not end here. In the weeks that followed, some of the women in dialogue with a facilitator continued to reflect on the issues raised by the study. They acknowledged to her that in beginning to appropriate the text, they needed to initiate dialogue on the matter with the male church leadership. They acknowledged that they needed to make choices concerning their church participation. They acknowledged their collusion. And so, perhaps the most significant effect has been the cognitive dissonance that has been created through the process of reading the text contextually. Surely it is this dissonance that will compel the disempowered to further action. After all, menstruation is a deeply private matter. It only takes one act of concealment to resist!

Works Consulted

African National Congress
1994   The Reconstruction and Development Programme. Johannesburg: Umanyano.

Agenda Collective
1995   "Gender Flaws in the RDP." Agenda: Empowering Women for Gender Equity 24:40–44.

Draper, Jonathan A. and Gerald O. West
1989   "Anglicans and Scripture in South Africa." Pp. 30–52 in *Bounty in Bondage*. Ed. Frank England and Torquil J. M. Paterson. Johannesburg: Ravan.

Philpott, Graham
1993   *Jesus is Tricky and God is Undemocratic: The Kin-dom of God in Amawoti*. Pietermaritzburg: Cluster.

West, Gerald O.
1993   *Contextual Bible Study*. Pietermaritzburg: Cluster.

1995   "The Dumb Do Speak: Articulating Incipient Readings of the Bible in Marginalized Communities." Pp. 174–92 in *The Bible in Ethics*. Ed. John W. Rogerson, Margaret Davies, and M. Daniel Carroll R. Sheffield: Sheffield Academic.

Wilson, Francis and Mampela Ramphele
1989   *Uprooting Poverty: The South African Challenge*. Johannesburg and Cape Town: David Philip.

POLARITY OR PARTNERSHIP?
RETELLING THE STORY OF MARTHA AND MARY
FROM ASIAN WOMEN'S PERSPECTIVE

Ranjini Rebera

ABSTRACT

For a patriarchal Asian church to hear the voices of women as initiators for change, we have to re-open doors that closed when Euro-centered education became the only vehicle for learning and research. Communication processes rooted in the culture of the people function as significant vehicles for initiating such change. This article focuses on the retelling of the Martha and Mary pericope from a South Asian story-telling perspective, with insights drawn from a series of women's workshops held in the region. It underscores the freedom and security that can be established to release women from androcentric interpretative processes that polarize women. It explores a model of partnership between two women disciples who were different yet equal, as a model for discipleship within the community of faith today.

INTRODUCTION

There is a story from a very conservative little village in Asia that goes like this: There once lived two sisters and a brother, whose parents had died. None of them was married, but the house they lived in was owned by the oldest of the three—a sister. As is the custom in South Asia she was the mother-figure in the home. She ran the home, made many of the decisions for the family, and was very protective of her younger sister and very supportive of her only brother. Because she was the owner of the house and property, she also had considerable status in the village community. She was considered to be a woman of means, as well as the real head of the family, though her brother was the figurative head of the family. In recent times this little family had become friends with another man. He traveled to many villages as a teacher and would make it a point to stop and visit this family whenever he passed through their village. At this point in our story, it appears that he was coming to dinner with the two sisters. Their brother was away from home and the two sisters were planning to entertain him to dinner.

The storyteller paused for response and reactions from the audience.

-93-

The first time I heard a similar introduction to a study of Luke 10:38–42 was at a South Asian Women's Leadership training workshop in Lahore, Pakistan. The storyteller and study leader was Christine Amjad Ali, a New Testament scholar from Pakistan. The responses she elicited from participants as she told this story, making pauses at significant points, reflected insights framed within South Asian culture and tradition (Amjad Ali: 144–46). Those responses included the following comments:

- "Single women would never invite an unmarried man into their home."
- "A single man would never accept an invitation to an unchaperoned dinner with unmarried sisters."
- "The women in the neighborhood would have a great deal to say to the sisters."
- "A good elder sister would never involve her younger sister in such a situation. It would reflect on her reputation."
- "Why did the brother not do something about the matter? What about his responsibility for his two sisters?"

The Method of Telling

The above responses came through the lens of South Asian tradition which is fairly clear-cut regarding the parameters of social behavior between women and men. The use of traditional storytelling techniques together with what Elisabeth Schüssler Fiorenza terms a "hermeneutic of suspicion" (1992:53) created the vehicle for retelling the story of Martha and Mary from an Asian perspective. My own experience in using a combination of these two methods to release women from androcentric interpretative processes has been both challenging and exciting. The process I use incorporates elements of all four stages of Schüssler Fiorenza's framework—suspicion, remembrance, proclamation, and creative actualization. It is, however, in the last stage of being able creatively to identify with the women in the biblical story by placing them side by side with our own experiences and identities that the participants in workshops have obtained the greatest degree of inspiration and learning.

Anecdotal storytelling has been an important element of communication strategies in Asia. The great religious texts of Hinduism and Buddhism contain epics that have become a part of the religious traditions of South Asia. Buddhist monks in ancient Sri Lanka used folktales to illustrate the teachings of the Buddha. These stories were later translated into Pali, the canonical language of Buddhism in South Asia, and included in the *Tipitaka*, which is the title given to the entire collection of the Buddhist canon. Within it is the *Therigatha*, which contains seventy-three poems composed by those Susan Murcott (3) calls "wise women of early Buddhism."

In modern Asia, teledramas are increasingly replacing oral storytelling sessions. Nevertheless the little groups that congregate around television sets in urban and rural Asia when teledramas (or "soaps" as they are called in western societies) are screened are indicators of an adult need for storytelling. Such instances become a form of symbolic language that brings families and communities together, especially communities of non-literate persons. The telling of the story becomes a vehicle for understanding attitudes, cultural taboos, relationships in family and kinship networks, and many patterns of social behavior.

For women, the telling of our stories has become a strong motif whenever and wherever we gather. It is now a significant communication ritual that establishes a safety net for exploring issues. Often our sense of identity is conveyed through this medium. At such moments our sense of authority is derived from the authorship of our stories and from the telling of our stories (Rebera, 1995a). Such methods of storytelling are now emerging in Asia as a vehicle for gaining new insights into the biblical text and for doing theology, especially among women. R. S. Sugirtharajah, an Asian theologian, uses the term "vernacular readings" to distinguish such non-formal hermeneutical approaches, which spring from within localized culture and communication processes, from "metropolitan readings" that assume a "working universality" (1994b:253).

The role of the storyteller is equally important to the process. The teller must blend with the story and be acceptable to the audience. Therefore, when a South Asian woman begins a Bible study with women from her own region, she is not only accepted as being one with them, but the responses and reactions she receives will contain not "merely the facts of the telling, but the feelings, the meanings, and the meaning-making" (Ramanujan: xx).

This pattern of storytelling as a part of the retelling of biblical texts is a developing tradition. In a series of workshops I directed and co-taught with three Asian feminist theologians, we used communication techniques that were indigenous to the different sub-regions of Asia to enable participants to feel safe in articulating their insights into the text (Rebera, 1995b:97–156). In such situations participants felt secure in abandoning traditional insights derived from Sunday school teachings, Sunday sermons, and conventional Bible study groups. Kwok Pui-lan, a leading Chinese feminist theologian writing on the importance of oral hermeneutics for Asian women, says:

> Bible study among Asian women is a communal event; they gather to talk about their own stories and the stories of the Bible, constructing new meanings and searching for wisdom for survival and empowerment. They treat the Bible as a living resource rather than an ancient text closed in itself. (44)

In the retelling of the Martha-Mary pericope as a South Asian story, participants in a Pakistan workshop spent a significant period of time in reconstructing a close bond that could have existed between the two sisters. Role playing was used to set the scene prior to Jesus' arrival in their home. Martha and Mary were portrayed as two sisters going about daily domestic rituals together. However, it was significant that through non-verbal strategies, the audience was made aware of a growing distancing between the two sisters. We sensed that Mary was gently but firmly pulling away from her "mother-figure" older sister. There were signs of a growing independence in Mary and a sense of loss of control and uncertainty in Martha. Martha's appeal to Jesus became the natural climax to a situation that both sisters felt needed the intervention of a member of the extended family. Jesus came across as the close family friend who would now fit into an extended family system, even though he did not share any blood-ties with them. He took on the mantle of a *anna* or *aiya* ("older brother" or "uncle")—terms of familiarity used to address unrelated males who are close family friends in South Asian communities.

A similar role-playing of this passage was done by a group that consisted of women and men from Africa and Latin America. Here both women were portrayed in a fairly stereotypical manner, with Mary fussing over what she should wear and how she would look while Martha was busily and noisily cleaning the house and making preparations for the visitor. The absence of a sense of safety within the group resulted in the escape to stereotyping. I am certain that should the method be used by an African storyteller with an African audience (or similarly in Latin America), the outcome would be very different.

One of the significant challenges faced by feminist Bible study leaders in Asia is to create avenues to enable Asian women to study and interpret the Bible, not as a written text alone, but as a book that was born out of oral traditions, similar to their own. As Kwok Pui-lan claims:

> When the Bible was introduced into Asia, it encountered a cultural world with different understandings of sacred texts and diverse modes of transmission. During the century of mission the Protestant missionaries who arrived to preach the Gospel in many parts of Asia were influenced by the print mentality of the western world and invariably understood *scripture* to be a written text. (47)

The use of creative, informal learning strategies becomes an even greater need when we respond to the reality that the majority of non-literate persons in Asia are women. However, since there is an elitist attitude to academic learning that continues to separate knowledge on the basis of the written text as opposed to oral communication, many women from rural and urban poor areas of Asia continue to feel incapable of doing theology since they do not have access to the written text. They lose sight of the fact that within Buddhism, Hinduism, Confucianism, and early Christian missionary activity scripture was transmitted through oral renditions, memorization, street theater, temple rituals and celebrations, dance, art and music. While working with a group of rural women workers in South India, I was struck by their eagerness to relate to information from written sources rather than to information drawn from rituals and customs within their own realities. These women worked among village women who had minimal education and therefore had no access to written materials. However, the devaluing of what was essentially a part of their identity as women from rural India and the valuing of an educated, middle-class identity as represented by myself created a climate of denial through the early days of the workshop. Only when I was able to create safe communication strategies that drew them away from print sources to explore issues within what were their own realities (such as a feminist reimaging of the Indian harvest festival, *Thaipongal*) did the workshop begin to move forward (Rebera, 1990).

Communal Bible studies for Asian women are more than intellectual exercises. They legitimize the need for women to come together to support each other, to hear each other's stories, to empower each other and to open "new doors and windows for seeing ourselves as Asian women, made in God's image" (Rebera, 1995b:97). Creating safe avenues for exploring scripture and doing theology will therefore give the silenced women of the Bible a voice and, at the same time, give women of today the freedom to claim their identity within their understanding of the message. Such understandings will also release Asian women to re-image their relationship with God and with community, in new and different ways.

RETELLING THE TEXT

In retelling the story of Mary and Martha in an international setting through the use of storytelling, the blending of stereotyped and traditional interpretations take precedence over regional and localized interpretations. Culture and social location are minimized within the desire to reach a globally acceptable interpretation. However, in this paper I will confine myself to South Asian insights into the text derived from interpretative processes I have created and used with Asian Bible study groups which are not bound by the constraints of a global hermeneutic.

a) *The setting.* When released from the constraints of traditional interpretations, women have raised interesting questions regarding the setting of this Lucan episode. For instance, since this story does not appear in any of the other three Gospels, where did the writer of Luke hear of it? As one woman observed, the content of the verses creates a conflict situation between two sisters. In Asian society such a situation would have remained a personal and private incident and would not be revealed to an outsider, particularly to any unrelated males. The text is clear that Jesus and his disciples were on the move, but the disciples seem to have disappeared during this encounter. Therefore, any form of rebuke of an older sister—if it was really a rebuke—would have stayed with the three concerned persons. How, then, would the writer have received an accurate account of what really transpired?

How would the teller's bias have influenced the retelling? This leads to the possibility that the writer needed to include an example that would point to the discipleship of women, within a chapter that dealt primarily with the training of disciples and their being dispatched in pairs to every town and village (Lk 10:1). The story of a *pair* of sisters in training as disciples then becomes a logical inclusion.

A group of women at another workshop introduced the element of choice when examining chapter 10 in its entirety. The issue of choice was portrayed as being of central importance in the instructions to the followers as they went in and out of towns. Choice was a central issue to the all-male cast in the parable of the good Samaritan that precedes the story of Martha and Mary. Choice was the focus of the Mary and Martha episode as each sister chose her own particular way of exercising and training for discipleship. When taken within the context of choice, Jesus' words to Martha reflected his affirmation of Mary's choice as being her right, rather than an elevation of one form of discipleship over another.

b) *Textual insights.* Although there is a wide acceptance of feminist interpretation as it comes out of the western academy, there is also a growing body of scholarship that is attempting to work within the feminist discipline as it comes out of the culture and the history of each Asian sub-region. Similar parallels are visible in South America and Africa. In her exploration of new understandings of theology from Asian women's perspectives, Korean theologian Chung Hyun Kyung emphasizes the collective and inclusive approach that women bring to creating theology (103–4). She observes:

> Asian women have expressed their theology through their prayers, songs, dances, devotional rituals, drawings, and the way they live in the community. They are the theologians who are carving out oral theology and non-verbal theology from body languages. The majority of such women have not received formal theological training from traditional educational institutions. (102)

V. 38: "Now as they went their way, he entered a certain village, where a woman named Martha welcomed him into her home."[1]

The ownership of property is an indicator of social standing and status in Asia. For women to be recognized as owners of property *despite the pres-*

---

[1] Unless otherwise indicated, all biblical citations are from the NRSV.

ence of a male sibling is a double affirmation of the woman, particularly in South Asia. She is regarded as the head of the home and also has authority and power in the community. In Sri Lanka, prior to the introduction of an uniform legal system by colonizers, Sinhala and Tamil law assured women of their right to inheritance and property. "Land remains an important asset for women from diverse social and economic backgrounds. . . . [T]he customary laws of Sri Lanka recognized the rights of women to own, acquire, manage and control their land. Patriarchal values based on Roman-Dutch Law filtered into Tamil (and Sinhala) customary law through judicial decisions and legislation" (Goonesekere). In postcolonial times the significance of Martha as an owner of property was subsumed in Martha, the traditional homemaker, as society now accepted the uniform legal system that placed women at a disadvantage where the ownership of property was concerned.

As the owner of her home despite the presence of a brother, Martha had the right to be viewed as a woman of authority who is also the head of a household. Such a view of Martha would make her an icon for authority, rather than an icon for home-making and serving, within the life of the church. Unfortunately, the more traditional view of Martha, as one who was tied to domesticity and who becomes the role model for women extending their domestic role into the life of the Church, continues to be the predominant image for most Asian women and men. Her status as a woman of means continues to be overshadowed by interpretations introduced by early missionaries and that continue to be in vogue today. When interpretations that reflect the status and role of women in western colonial countries (reinforced by patriarchal attitudes and theology) are hidden behind a text, they perpetuate such outdated patterns of behavior for women, especially where ownership of property and ownership of women intertwine. It is also a conveniently forgotten fact that women in countries that were once the colonizers no longer subscribe to many of these images for participation in church and society. "Consequently many women in the church, who even now tend to identify with Martha, feel that they are less valuable, even worthless, and develop inferiority complexes" (Moltmann-Wendel: 21).

V. 39: "She had a sister named Mary, who sat at the Lord's feet and listened to what he was saying."

The interpretation of this verse has been used to legitimize the role of women in church ministry. All translations create the image of Mary, the silent listener, taking full advantage of Jesus' visit to learn from him. She continues to be the icon for women's participation in the church as the adoring, silent receiver of the Word. The Korean feminist theologian Chung Sook Ja writes: "Korean women are taught that the life of Mary is the life in the church: sitting close to Jesus means to sit in the worship room, close to the pulpit; to listen to Jesus means to study the Bible with the pastor" (1992:248).

Many feminist scholars draw attention to Mary as a disciple sitting with her teacher. The Norwegian feminist scholar Turid Karlsen Seim claims:

> Mary sitting at the Lord's feet and listening to his words is portrayed in the typical position of the pupil (cf. Acts 22:3). The description of a teacher-pupil relationship is an important feature of the text. The role as student in which Mary is positioned goes beyond the normal opportunity for women to hear the word in the context of worship. Moreover the text alludes to terms that in rabbinic tradition are connected to teaching institutions. (745–46)

In her examination of social conflict centered around meals and meal preparation in the Synoptic traditions, Kathleen Corley draws attention to the meal being prepared by Martha, and Mary's posture and position at the feet of Jesus as that of "a traditional, silent wife" (137) as more relevant to the reading of this text than would be the interpretation of Mary as a rabbinical student. The latter suggestion, however, resonates with the perceptions of Amjad Ali in her interpretation of Mary "sitting at the feet" of Jesus.

> What does "sitting at the feet" mean? In India and Pakistan this phrase is used to describe a particular relationship between a teacher (*guru*) and a disciple (*sishya*). . . .According to this tradition, when Mary sat at Jesus' feet she was staking her claim to be a disciple of Jesus. She indicates that she wishes to learn from him so she could become *a teacher herself one day*. When Jesus begins to teach Mary he acknowledges that he recognizes her as a disciple-in-training, similar to the role being played by the twelve male disciples. (145)

The concept of *guru* (teacher) and *sishya* (student) has deep historical roots in South Asia. It goes beyond the absorption of knowledge for the sake of learning alone. Hindu religious codes as reflected in *The Law of Manu* make specific references to behavior codes between the *guru* and the *sishya*. Manisha Roy, a Bengali anthropologist, explores the concept in Hinduism:

> The ideal behavior for the disciple is the same for both male and female. The disciple should address a *guru* as *bàbà* (father) and treat him respectfully and with utter obedience; the *guru* must treat the disciple with affection, guidance and understanding. He (the *guru*) becomes not just a religious teacher, but a guide, a friend, and a father to the disciple because he is guiding the disciple to be with the god and attain ultimate salvation. (168–69)

Buddhism too had its share of *gurus* and *sishyas*. Buddhist feminist scholars are researching and retelling the stories of women who were disciples of the Buddha and who went on to form their own orders within Buddhism and become teachers themselves. Foremost among such women was the

Buddhist nun Pajapati, whose disciples became the first ordained Buddhist nuns about the sixth century B.C.E. (Murcott: 31–56). Murcott observes further that "the model that the nuns of the *Therigatha* provide is one where women have the capacity to realize and understand the highest religious goals of their faith in the same roles and to the same degree as men" (10).

Many South Asian women have "sat at the feet" of a *guru* in recent years. After completing the required period of apprenticeship they have gone on to be *gurus* themselves. A well-known *guru* in India was Pandit Ramabhai, an educated Brahmin woman. She did her apprenticeship guided by her father Ananta Shastri, and later went on to form the first home for widows in the Indian State of Maharashtra (Kumar: 26). Mahatma Gandhi, the well-known Indian *guru*, encouraged both female and male disciples to follow his teachings. Many of his women disciples went on to become activists in India's struggle for freedom from Britain. Gandhi claimed, "It is given to her (woman) to teach the art of peace to the warring world thirsting for that nectar. She can become the leader in *satyagraha* (non-violence) which does not require the learning that books give but does require the stout heart that comes from suffering and death" (Kumar: 82).

The tradition of women as disciples going on to be teachers and leaders is culturally acceptable in South Asian society. When viewed from this standpoint, Mary ceases to be a silent receiver. She becomes an active participant in a training process that extended to Jesus' male disciples as well. Mary makes her choice as to the form of her apprenticeship that will lead her into her role as a *guru* or a teacher.

V. 40: "But Martha was distracted by her many tasks; so she came to him and asked, 'Lord, do you not care that my sister has left me to do all the work by myself? Tell her then to help me.'"

Asian women are sometimes puzzled by this verse. It does not quite fit the accepted behavior codes between two sisters and an unrelated male. It becomes doubly puzzling for South Asian women when they equate Jesus to the pastor or priest in the local church. For them it would be unthinkable to air any family disagreement in such a public manner. A workshop participant from Bangladesh made the observation that should she have any complaints about her sister she *may* see her pastor privately and ask for advice on how to deal with a "lazy" sister. Her first preference would be to go to another woman in the family circle rather than to a male outsider. What was more difficult to accept was the offering of hospitality combined with a complaint about behavior and then expecting the honored guest to arbitrate in the matter!

A further observation related to Mary's silence in the face of Martha's words was that in Asian culture it was most probable that the younger sister would not challenge her older sister in the presence of an outsider. She would remain silent and perhaps challenge her sister at a more private time. Manisha Roy, in examining the many relationships between family and kinship networks, writes of the daughter-mother relationship that the daughter "must respect and obey her mother and mother-figures (paternal aunts, older classificatory siblings) while listening to what they instruct her about her future life" (156; see also Rebera, 1995b:43–60, 77–95). Martha as the mother-figure in the family would fit the role of "older classificatory sibling," and, given that role, Mary would hesitate to be disrespectful towards her older sister. Hence Mary's silence.

Vv. 41–42: "But the Lord answered her, 'Martha, Martha, you are worried and distracted by many things; there is need of only one thing. Mary has chosen the better part, which will not be taken away from her.'"

The encounter between Jesus and the two sisters climaxes with Jesus' words to Martha that are traditionally interpreted to favor Mary's stance of contemplative discipleship as being of a higher category than Martha's which was reflected in "fretting and fussing about so many things" (NEB). Jesus' response has been used to validate women's participation in the church as one of silence and women's spirituality as derived from an unquestioning dependence on Christ.

The difficulty in reconstructing this verse from a feminist perspective is reflected in the many articles and chapters written by feminist scholars about this encounter. Jesus' use of the words "chosen the better part" has challenged feminist scholars in the rereading of this text. An important factor in the understanding of these words has been the need to eliminate the polarization of women's ministries that has been caused by male-centered theology based on these verses.

A role-play of this pericope by a group of Indian women led to significant insights. Once again the sisters had been portrayed as being in a close sibling relationship. Both Martha and Mary were portrayed as disciples-in-training. This factor gave each sister the independent right to seek approval from their *guru*, Jesus. Therefore, when Jesus responded to Martha he was not seen as pitting one sister against the other, but as supporting Mary in her choice with what was best for her. He was accepting of Mary's desire to be different in her apprenticeship. He was also seen as understanding of Martha's "mother-figure" concern for the welfare of her younger sister. Martha's worry and distraction were connected to the reputation of the younger sister. Christine Amjad Ali observed, "Perhaps we think that Jesus was walking around with a halo on his head and that everyone would know that he was the wonderful Son of God! But he did not. He was an ordinary Asian man in an Asian country who was a good friend to these two sisters and their brother" (144). Jesus' response was seen as an assurance that being apprenticed to him was "a better thing" than following the traditional dictates of society that often confined and limited women in public and private roles.

In South Asian culture for a woman to remain unmarried after the age of twenty years is often a reflection of an inadequacy on the part of the woman as well as her parents. In the case of two unmarried sisters, with no parent in evidence, this would be an even greater burden. To break such societal barriers and to become a *sishya* to an unmarried male is to compound the negative attitudes extended to such a family. In the discussion that followed this role-play, many drew attention to the role of unmarried women in ministry in India. In the Protestant churches they are viewed as being "different" from women who are wives and mothers. Single women in ministry are often pitied as being unable to fulfill their obligations as a woman, which is to marry and have children. In a rapidly developing technological India, singleness among women is growing. The right to choose marriage and/ or a profession is becoming a visible phenomenon in urban, middle-class India. Therefore, the issue of the status of single women is becoming a focus for discussion and debate. Viewing these verses from the perspective of single women, choosing to build their own journeys in their own manner, and reading Jesus' response as a validation of that right, adds weight to the argument that the right of choice is not a gender-based prerogative but a human right.

Partnership not Polarity

The focus in all the retellings I have participated in has been on the two sisters as the central figures in the story, rather than on Jesus or his response to Martha's words. This emphasis falls easily into the structure of chapter 10 as it deals with the choice of men and women to be disciples, how this choice is exercised, and the sending out of the seventy in pairs. The re-telling of this pericope from an Asian perspective is imperative if Asian church women are to be released from androcentric interpretations that continue to polarize women, define women's ministry, and hold us captive within kyriarchal traditions. Gao Ying from China writes:

> In traditional Chinese biblical interpretation, women are led to believe that they should try to be Christians like Mary but not Martha. But here the analysis shows that the Chinese church also needs "Marthas" to peform administrative affairs. As a matter of fact there are many "Marthas" today in the Chinese church who are making contributions to the church's ministry. (60)

Chung Sook Ja from Korea claims:

> Many Korean male pastors understand Martha as a woman who was involved in many activities outside of her church, and Mary as a woman who dedicated herself to work in her own church. They emphasize that, because Martha's attitude was not welcomed by Jesus, church women should not be

active in many things outside of their churches and should, rather, work in their local churches. (1993:19)

The Asian feminist perspectives presented here are by no means the norm in Asia. They are a part of a branch of feminist scholarship that is still in its infancy. They are indicative of the struggle for Asian scholarship to establish its own genre in the field of biblical scholarship. For Asian women retelling biblical texts from our own realities has great significance.

- It places the culture of biblical women side by side with the culture of Asian women. This enables us to see the similarities between socio-cultural attitudes and expectations of women as they existed in Hebrew society and in Asia today. It moves us away from the written text to the exploration of those realities that are common to women in both settings. Once we begin our search for meaning from this position, we see the events and characters in the Bible as persons we can relate to, rather than as events that are used to be prescriptive regarding our attitudes and behavior as Christian women.
- Episodes such as the Martha and Mary pericope assist in reclaiming Asian traditions that have been lost through influences from outside the region. Concepts of discipleship that expressed an accepted role for women in Asian religious practice can be reintroduced to add deeper meaning to the claims of women for a discipleship of equals in a kyriarchal church. Such a process moves Mary from the foot of the pulpit to the position of an equal.
- Such study moves the focus from polarizing women in the church to one of partnership. It eradicates the "Martha-or-Mary" stereotype and replaces it with understandings of "Martha—the disciple" and "Mary—the disciple" working in partnership with each other and with Jesus. This concept is developed further by Chung Sook Ja of Korea who explores Jesus' partnership with Mary and Martha as "Women becoming Disciples for Partnership," claiming:

> I want to develop women's liberation into the action in community by inter-
> preting this story as an example of Jesus' new community in partnership.
> Jesus' declaration about "the most important part" should be understood
> from the perspective of partnership. For Jesus the role distinction was not
> a big issue, but the broken partnership between Mary and Martha was.
> (1992:251)

- For a patriarchal Asian church to hear the voice of women as initiators for change, we have to re-open doors that closed or were half-closed when Euro-centered education became accepted as the only vehicle for learning and research. Communication processes rooted in the culture of the people need to be used as a significant vehicle for initiating such change.

• In cultures where women's identity continues to be derived from our relationship to a male figure, be it a father, husband, brother, uncle, or male priest, it becomes an urgent task to release women from such a loss of identity. It is through the reclaiming of our identity as Asian women who are different from each other, as Martha and Mary were different, that we can claim the right to be equal in all aspects of discipleship and the right to be equal partners within the community of faith.

WORKS CONSULTED

Amjad Ali, Christine
 1995   "Role Models for the New Community: Mary and Martha." Pp. 143–47
           in *Affirming Difference, Celebrating Wholeness: A Partnership of Equals*. Ed.
           Ranjini Rebera. Hong Kong: Christian Conference of Asia.

Chung Hyun Kyung
 1990   *Struggle to be the Sun Again: Introducing Asian Women's Theology*. Mary-
           knoll, NY: Orbis.

Chung Sook Ja
 1992   "Bible Study from the Perspective of Korean Feminist Theology." Ph.D.
           diss., San Francisco Theological Seminary.

 1993   "Women's Discipleship for Partnership." *In God's Image* 12.1:18–20.

Corley, Kathleen E.
 1993   *Private Women, Public Meals: Social Conflict in the Synoptic Tradition*.
           Peabody: Hendrickson.

Fabella, Virginia and Park Sun Ai Lee, eds.
 1989   *We Dare to Dream: Doing Theology as Asian Women*. Hong Kong: Asian
           Women's Resource Centre.

Fabella, Virginia and Mercy Amba Oduyoye, eds.
 1988   *With Passion and Compassion: Third World Women Doing Theology*. Mary-
           knoll, NY: Orbis.

Gao Yin
 1994   "Martha and Mary's Relationship with Jesus from a Feminist Perspec-
           tive." *In God's Image* 13.1:60–63.

Goonesekere, Savitri W. E.
 1989   "Mobilizing Law in Improving Economic Status of Women." Pp. F1–F32
           in "Women as Economic Producers—Challenges to Policymakers."
           Colombo: Institute of Policy Studies, unpublished papers.

King, Ursula, ed.
 1994   *Feminist Theology from the Third World: A Reader*. Maryknoll, NY: Orbis.

Kinukawa, Hisako
1994   Women and Jesus in Mark: A Japanese Feminist Perspective.. Maryknoll, NY: Orbis.

Kumar, Radha
1993   The History of Doing: An Illustrated Account of Movements for Women's Rights and Feminism in India. New Delhi: Kali For Women.

Kwok Pui-lan
1995   Discovering the Bible in the Non-Biblical World. Maryknoll, NY: Orbis.

Moltmann-Wendel, Elisabeth
1988   The Women Around Jesus. New York: Crossroad.

Murcott, Susan
1991   The First Buddhist Women: Translations and Commentary on the Therigatha. Berkeley: Parallax.

Ortega, Ofelia, ed.
1995   Women's Visions: Theological Reflection, Celebration, Action. Geneva: World Council of Churches.

Ramanujan, A. K.
1991   Folktales from India: A Selection of Oral Tales from Twenty-two Languages. New York: Pantheon.

Rebera, Ranjini
1990   A Search for Symbols: An Asian Experiment. Hong Kong: Christian Conference of Asia.

1995a   A Partnership of Equals, A Resource Guide for Asian Women. Hong Kong: Christian Conference of Asia.

Rebera, Ranjini, ed.
1995b   Affirming Difference, Celebrating Wholeness: A Partnership of Equals. Hong Kong: Christian Conference of Asia.

Roy, Manisha
1993   Bengali Women. Chicago: University of Chicago Press.

Sanneh, Lamin
1993   Encountering the West: Christianity and the Global Cultural Process. Maryknoll, NY: Orbis.

Schüssler Fiorenza, Elisabeth
1985   In Memory of Her: A Feminist Theological Reconstruction of Christian Origins. New York: Crossroad.

1992   But She Said: Feminist Practices of Biblical Interpretation. Boston: Beacon.

Schüssler Fiorenza, Elisabeth, ed.
1993   Searching the Scriptures: A Feminist Introduction. Vol 1. New York: Crossroad.

1994   *Searching the Scriptures: A Feminist Commentary. Vol 2.* New York: Crossroad.

Seim, Turid Karlsen
1994   "The Gospel of Luke." Pp. 728–62 in *Searching the Scriptures: A Feminist Commentary. Vol. 2.* Ed. Elisabeth Schüssler Fiorenza. New York: Crossroad.

Sugirtharajah, R. S.
1994b   "Introduction and Some Thoughts on Asian Biblical Hermeneutics." *BibInt* 2:251–63.

Sugirtharajah, R. S., ed.
1991   *Voices From the Margin: Interpreting the Bible in the Third World.* Maryknoll, NY: Orbis (first edition).

1993   *Asian Faces of Jesus.* Maryknoll, NY: Orbis.

1994a   *Frontiers in Asian Christian Theology: Emerging Trends.* Maryknoll, NY: Orbis.

A KOREAN FEMINIST READING OF JOHN 4:1-42

Jean K. Kim
Vanderbilt University

ABSTRACT

This paper approaches the dialogue between Jesus and the Samaritan woman in John 4 from a Korean feminist perspective, and shows not only how the text has traditionally been used by male power for the oppression of women in a colonialist situation, but also how the Samaritan woman herself was constrained by the Gospel writer into the role of exchange object between groups of men. This "ethical reading" removes this story from the hands of those who have used it for the oppression of women and restores it to the victimized as a means and a direction for their liberation.

INTRODUCTION

The song "Fill my cup, Lord," based on John 4, is one of the famous songs sung in Korean-American churches located around military bases in the U.S. At these churches, Korean women who followed their GI husbands to America, and who find themselves culturally isolated and regarded by their communities as immoral women, are told the story of the Samaritan woman. Through that story these women learn that even though the Samaritan woman had more than five husbands, they brought her no satisfaction. Then, one day, she came to meet Jesus at the well and heard about a real spring of living water gushing up into eternal life. The ministers then draw a parallel between these women's situation and that of the Samaritan woman which is intended to reinforce the identification of these women as sinners. Such an abrupt identification of these Korean Army brides, who often divorce and re-marry many times, with the Samaritan woman leads me to read John 4:1-42 closely. I question not only why the Samaritan woman had to have more than five husbands, but also how the unquestioned authority of the Bible has ignored women's subjectivity in biblical times as well as nowadays. This contextual situation of the Korean women who married American GIs makes me recognize the necessity of an "ethical reading" of the Bible, by which I mean, first, an inclusive reading that discovers the voice of the marginalized in the text as well as in a context and, second, a critical reading that reveals the problematic norm of Western scholarship that regards the text as a historical object. This ethical reading will make possible a critique of the view of Western scholarship that regards John 4 as a good example of mission or of women's discipleship but does not pay attention to the Samaritan woman's seemingly immoral life, and thus fails to recognize the oppressive function of that story in the relationship of colonial powers to women in the Third World, especially during the colonial periods.

The Bible has its location within history in a certain culture. It is not static but rather in motion when it is read by a flesh and blood reader. Therefore, the ethical reading of the Bible should be responsible not only to the biblical text but also to the others who face the Bible in their context. With the task of an ethical reading of the Bible in mind, and reading John 4 from a Korean feminist perspective, I will first show the parallel between the Samaritan woman and these Korean women in terms of their victimization during colonial periods, and in so doing, I will clarify how Western interpretations of John 4 have impacted women in the non-Western world, including those women who find themselves trapped in a kind of cultural limbo around U.S. military bases. Then, to pursue the ethical reading of this text, I will suggest a *Minjung* feminist interpretation based on a real context, which can not only console the *Han* of those women[1] but also free the Samaritan woman from centuries of voiceless enslavement to an interpretation of the text that served to further the essentially imperialistic nature of male constructed power.

THE VICTIMIZATION OF THE SAMARITAN WOMAN

The dialogue between Jesus and the Samaritan woman in John's Gospel has been favored by people of the Third World and women because of the interpretation that through this dialogue Jesus broke ethnic, religious, gender, and moral barriers (Rodriguez: 420–26; Hogan: 63–69; Schneiders: 35–45). However, if we approach this text as a rhetorical narrative in which social, cultural, and ideological perspectives are imbedded, we find that such a romantic interpretation of the text can only bring about an unacceptable ideology for a pluralistic society.

There are two strangers, a Samaritan woman and a Jewish man, at the well. By setting the dialogue between Jesus and the Samaritan woman in the betrothal type-scene which is familiar to his/her reader (Gen 24:10–61; 29:1–20; Exod 2:15–21), the author of John's Gospel leads his/her readers into understandable expectations of the meeting between Jesus and the Samaritan woman. The dialogue between Jesus and the woman begins with Jesus' request for water. The Samaritan woman's response, "How is it you, a Jew,

---

1 The Korean word *Minjung* means the grassroots people who are politically oppressed, socially marginalized, economically exploited, and kept uneducated; *Han* means the wounded mind and heart of the *Minjung*.

ask a drink of me, a woman of Samaria?" shows that the dialogue between Jesus and the woman is not like the betrothal type-scene where the women is passive or silent in response to the man's request. Rather it shows that she is caught in a dilemma: as a woman, she should respond humbly to the request of a higher status male, but as a Samaritan woman she should not talk to a Jew. Regardless of the point of the Samaritan woman's question, Jesus answers her question in terms of his own identity, not in terms of the relationship between a Samaritan woman and a Jewish man. Also, instead of getting water from her as he asked, without asking if she needs it or not, Jesus proceeds to offer her the living water (v. 10). Since Jesus' offering of living water is so abrupt, she raises a question again; "From where?" Like the earlier question, "How is it?" (v. 9), the woman's question "From where?" indeed reflects a much deeper ignorance on her part. Jesus undercuts her questions again by emphasizing the superiority of the water which he is offering (vv. 13–14).

It may be said that the dialogue between Jesus and the Samaritan woman is developed on the basis of an irony whose function is to reveal Jesus' identity as a messiah, because the contrast between Jesus' omniscient knowledge and the ignorance or false assumption of the woman is highlighted throughout the dialogue. According to Gail O'Day (1986:31–32), the ironic structure of this story intends to give a reader an omniscient vantage point from which to perceive the Samaritan woman's misunderstanding. At the narrative level, the irony or the misunderstanding of the Samaritan woman makes it clear that the author of John's Gospel succeeds in communicating with his/her reader. Since the reader can receive what the Samaritan woman does not, the author and the reader are in accord with Jesus. J. E. Botha (130–31) agrees with O'Day that the readers know what Jesus refers to, and thus the irony of the Samaritan woman's words reaches its climax when she misunderstands Jesus' sayings and takes them in a literal sense.

Indeed, the author of John's Gospel never allows the Samaritan woman to grasp the meaning of Jesus' saying, but rather he/she simply uses her ignorance or misunderstanding for the purpose of the progressive revelation of Jesus' identity. By attributing the ironic force of the narrative to the author of John's Gospel, O'Day restricts the text to a simple reading subject. However, the text itself is not stable but is disruptive enough to sustain a certain independence over against every reader according to his/her situation: a contemporary reader's experience can work in the text to draw a different meaning from the same text. In other words, the textual irony provides a reader with the ethical challenge based on a certain context to seek multidimensional meanings in the Samaritan woman's story.

Such an ethical challenge brings about another aspect of the text, which is different from a simple textual irony. The author of John's Gospel makes the Samaritan woman into an unimportant "other" by seeking to silence her, with her only purpose being the revelation of Jesus' identity. In light of this, the term "victimization" is much more suitable than the term "irony." A further developed victimization of the Samaritan woman is easily seen in the rest of the story. Without a direct comment on the woman's perception of the living water, Jesus suddenly changes the topic of their conversation. Jesus' abrupt mention of her husband is unexpected because apparently her husband has nothing to do with the living water. It might have been considered immoral for a woman to marry more than five times. (In fact, Brown [171] observes that according to Jewish custom a woman could marry only three times.) However, the implication of her immoral life is not developed, nor are we given anything but the bare details about her marital status. The mention of her immoral life thus simply serves the purpose of revealing Jesus' identity: Jesus' omniscient intuition that she had five husbands and is now living with a man who is not her husband makes her confess that Jesus is a prophet. In short, at the cost of her shameful past, Jesus' identity is gradually revealed.

Just because the Samaritan woman recognizes Jesus as a prophet, some may say that she reveals Jesus' identity, vocation, and the nature of faithful discipleship (O'Day, 1992:294). Yet, a further reading of the rest of the story does not allow us to accept what is, again, a romantic view. As soon as she confesses that Jesus is a prophet, she shifts the topic from Jesus' identity to the proper place of worship, which suggests that she still does not fully grasp his identity. For the first time, Jesus responds to her question seriously (v. 21; cf. vv. 10, 13, 16). Here, however, he does not simply answer her but rather advances the issue. Whereas the woman simply mentions the worship place, Jesus enlarges the topic to include the object of the worship. By negating the distinction between the worship places, Jesus seems to dissolve the tension between the Samaritans and Jews, to which they have clung. But, in fact, the Samaritan woman is ignored again by Jesus' utterance that Samaritans worship what they do not know (v. 22), by his affirmation of Jewish superiority to the Samaritans, and by her inability to recognize Jesus as the real Messiah (v. 25). Jesus' identity as Messiah is not revealed by the woman but by Jesus himself, as the expression ἐγώ εἰμι ("I am") shows. In this way, the Samaritan woman plays the role of a vehicle by which Jesus' identity is further revealed. Therefore, the woman cannot be a revealer of Jesus in a real sense, but is rather a victim of the author of John's Gospel, and on the narrative level, a victim of Jesus.

So far, the Samaritan woman has been victimized by a foreign man—a Jew—but her victimization does not end here. As soon as she hears Jesus' self-revelation, she goes directly to her town and proclaims what she saw and heard from Jesus, and then she brings people to Jesus. Because of her contribution in bringing her people to Jesus, it is possible to think that the woman shows a true discipleship in the sense that she contributes to a mission. By using "meanwhile," however, the author of John's Gospel inserts the dialogue between Jesus and his disciples in order to address the role of Jesus' disciples. With that literary insertion, the direct response of her people to her witness is replaced by the dialogue between Jesus and his disciples (vv. 31–38), where Jesus' disciples are shown as the "harvesters" of large numbers of converts to which the author of John's Gospel had alluded before (vv. 1–2). In short, the replacement of the direct response of her people to the Samaritan woman's witness by the dialogue between Jesus and his disciples shows that the woman is not a missionary but a victimized woman whose purpose is to exemplify the role of exchange object between groups of men. This role becomes clear at the end of the narrative. After intercalating the dialogue between Jesus and his disciples, the author of John's Gospel swiftly introduces the Samaritan people's coming to Jesus. What the Samaritan woman said to her people is not clear, but the author of John's Gospel shows that her people come to believe in Jesus because of her saying (v. 38). However, after they once meet and stay with Jesus, they deny that they believed in Jesus because of her saying, but attribute their belief to their own experience of Jesus (v. 42). Here, the Samaritan woman is cut down again even by her people instead of being appreciated (vv. 39–42). Despite the fact that the woman brings her people to Jesus and causes them to confess that Jesus is "the savior of the world," she is not approved even once by Jesus or by her people. Rather, she exemplifies thoroughly the role of exchange object between groups of men.

Thus, from the above reading of the Samaritan woman's story, I do not find any important role for the Samaritan woman as a revealer of Jesus, a missionary, or a disciple. Also, I do not discover who the Samaritan woman was, why she had to have more than five husbands, or why her tragic or seemingly sinful life had to be mentioned in this story. She is not developed as an important character nor allowed to have justification for her string of husbands, but rather, she is simply used as a medium to reveal Jesus' identity and his disciples' mission. As a woman reader, however, I cannot help paying attention to how the Samaritan woman has been considered a representative of immoral or sinful women in patriarchal society. More concretely, as a Korean woman reader who has heard the crying of the suffering Korean women during the colonial periods, I have no interest in Jesus' identity or his mission any more. Rather, I am concerned with the Samaritan woman's life, and why she had to have more than five husbands despite the patriarchal convention which considered her an immoral woman.

At this point, Craig R. Koester's claims deserve my attention. Borrowing from the tendency of the Old Testament to depict the religious apostasy of Israel in terms of a woman's sexual unfaithfulness (cf. Hos 2:2, 7, 16; Jer 2:1–13), the author of John's Gospel might have described the Samaritan woman as a representative of the Samaritan people who are not faithful to

God. The Samaritan nation originated when five foreign nations settled with their pagan deities in Samaria after the fall of the northern kingdom (2 Kgs 17:24, 29–31). On the basis of this convention, interpreters have suggested that the Samaritan woman's marital infidelity stands for the religious infidelity of the Samaritan people (Olsson: 184; Carmichael: 332–46). Against this allegorical interpretation, Koester suggests a socio-politically oriented interpretation. In order to support his thesis, he insists that the allegorical interpretation is not only alien to John's Gospel but also inconsistent with 2 Kgs 17:30–31, where five foreign nations and seven pagan deities are mentioned (1990:669–70). Also, the allegorical interpretation which goes back to the origin of the Samaritan nation is not plausible because the author of John's Gospel deals with the first-century disputes between Jews and Samaritans. Rather, considering the tendency of the author of John's Gospel to utilize an individual as a spokesperson for a large group, Koester claims that the Samaritan woman's personal history parallels her national history, which has been under colonial domination since the Assyrian occupation brought five foreign nations into Samaria. The Jews thus regarded the Samaritans as the descendants of these colonists, with whom they had intermarried in earlier times. But the Samaritans did not intermarry with foreigners when they were under the control of Herod the Great. With this socio-political explanation, Koester suggests that "the woman's personal history of marriage to five husbands and cohabitation with a sixth parallels the colonial history of Samaria" (1995:49). Considering the fact that the dialogue between the Samaritan woman and Jesus is presented as a plural form of speech (vv. 12, 20, 22), it is highly possible that the woman's personal history stands for the history of Samaria. Also, his claim that "the Savior of the world," which is not a typical messianic designation in the first-century Jewish or Samaritan thought, is intended to show disregard for the Roman imperial power supports his thesis that the five husbands and the sixth man of the Samaritan woman are the foreign colonists which have occupied Samaria (1990:665).

Unlike the previous interpretations, Koester's seems insightful and convincing. His conclusion cannot be overstated, namely, that Jesus' abrupt comment that the Samaritan woman had more than five men may mean that she was a victim throughout the colonial periods, which themselves were the product of an ideological power game between nations, both literally (men/women) and symbolically (colonist/Samaria). However, Koester does not further analyze the relationship between the Samaritan woman's personal life and the history of Samaria in such a way as to show how the colonial power impacted on women's lives. Such a victimization of the Samaritan woman by colonial powers reminds me of the situation of Korean women during the colonial periods, including the period of so-called neo-colonialism by Western nations and Western culture.

KOREAN WOMEN DURING THE COLONIAL PERIODS

Like Samaria, Korea has lived under colonialism. As a small country, whose origin goes back to 2335 B.C.E. when Tangun founded Korea, Korea has suffered from the domination of foreign powers since Korean recorded history began. Before the Japanese invasions, there were many conflicts between Korea and China. After the end of the Goryo dynasty, many Korean women were taken as hostages by the Chinese.[2] However, the most tragic and incurable suffering in the history of Korean women began with Japanese colonization. Under Japanese colonization, the soul and body of Korean women were totally violated by the Japanese military. During World War II, Japan recruited Korean women at random as sexual objects for Japanese soldiers in the battlefields.[3] Countless women died of venereal disease or were killed by Japanese soldiers because of their refusal to have sexual intercourse.[4] After the war was over, the few women who survived this hell could not return to Korea because they were ashamed of themselves, so they killed themselves or lived as hermits in the Japanese countryside without disclosing their identity.

However, this tragic suffering did not end with Korean independence from Japan, for we had to exchange liberation from Japanese imperialism for the division of our country. At the end of World War II, the two competing superpower nations, the U.S.S.R. and the U.S.A., insisted on the division of our small country to advance their own military strategies. Their political and military competition in the region brought about the Korean war, which resulted in the division of Korea, but also helped Japan recover from her defeat in World War II. Even after the Korean war was over, the two superpowers' militaries involved themselves in both South and North Korea, with the result that "the two Koreas now rank as fifth and sixth in military might in the world, with nuclear weapons in stock to be used at any time" (Manan-

---

2 The sexist word "Hwa Nyang Nyun," which means "a loose woman" or "wanton," originated from "Hwan Hyang Nyun," which means a woman who came back home from her life as a hostage in China (Han: 72).

3 There would have been about 139,000 "comfort women," who were forcibly recruited from young village girls across Asia. It is estimated that eighty percent of them were Korean women, because they were preferred by the soldiers after Japanese and Okinawan women. A major obstacle to obtaining a clearer picture of the recruitment process in Korea has been the shortage of official records of draft procedures. All such documentation was systematically destroyed at the end of the war, as was the case with all confidential material that could be used as evidence in war crimes trials. Even until now, the Japanese Education Ministry hides the atrocities committed during Japanese colonial rule in Korea and has kept any reference to comfort women out of the nation's textbooks (Hicks: 11–49).

4 A comfort woman had to service thirty to forty men daily, with the largest number coming on Sundays when the men were off duty (Hicks: 50–51).

zan and Park: 81). Because of this, Korean women have come to face another aspect of suffering.

The victimized women's case after the Korean war is different from the case of those who suffered under Japanese colonialism. Just as Japanese soldiers were greedy for their sexual objects, U.S. soldiers also needed theirs. Raping Korean women or visiting them in whore houses around the bases, American GIs have been able to gratify their sexual desires.[5] Yet, American GIs could avoid being criticized by the Korean people because of successful American propaganda which portrays America as a liberating force in the Korean war and as an indispensable peacemaker through its current military presence in South Korea. What is worse, since this propaganda cooperated with anti-communist ideology to support the Korean military government whose main interest lies in the economic development of the country, the target of people's criticism has not been American GIs but rather those women who are their victims.[6]

Whether these women were raped or were forced by social or economic pressure to become prostitutes, the result of their lives is the same—desperation and anger, or a feeling of betrayal. In the event that they had children whose fathers were American GIs, they had to endure shame and ridicule in a homogeneous society where intermarriage is regarded as a shameful thing. So, their lives and their children's lives were full of tears and shame, and they could not have any hopeful future in Korea. Some of these women, who considered themselves lucky, could come to America with their husbands. Yet, no sooner had they arrived in America than they felt frustration because of linguistic, ethnic, and cultural barriers. As a result, they became dependent on their husbands who often did not care about their situation at

---

5 In this vein, the records of the Army's World War II convictions for rape show that more than two-thirds of the convictions took place, not during the war itself, but during the occupation. So, too, Vietnamese women became occupational prostitutes as a direct result of the foreign military presence in their country. In such circumstances, however, the military may try its rapists on lesser charges, such as assault with intent to commit rape. The Army judiciary could give us no statistics on the number of convictions for these lesser charges, nor could they give us the number of reported rapes, arrests, and rape cases brought to trial. According to the available information on rape convictions in Vietnam, among 971 rape convictions, only fifty-two soldiers were executed. An additional eighteen men (not included among the 971) were executed after a combined conviction for rape and murder. Considering the fact that, despite the smaller size of U.S. peak troop concentrations in Korea (394,000 men) than in Vietnam (543,400 men), there were more convictions in Korea from May 31, 1951, to May 30, 1953, than in Vietnam during a two-year period, it is possible to conclude that the rape rate was higher per soldier in Korea (Brownmiller: 75–99).

6 These women are estimated at about one million. This indicates that the principal victims of the political-military and socio-economic subordination of separated Korea are the powerless women. Nevertheless, the problem of prostitution has not received attention from the public. This public negligence is largely due to the privatization of prostitution, or to the fact that the society sees it as a matter of the moral corruption of the individual prostitute (Park: 41–49).

all. The more they became dependent on their husbands, the more serious their situation became. Furthermore, regardless of their attempts to adjust to life in a foreign country, in many cases their husbands suddenly left them, and they fell into desperation again.

This desperation is usually manifested in one of two ways: either they fall into insanity, or they repeat the cycle of marriage and divorce. In the worst cases, their choice is between suicide and having many husbands like the Samaritan woman in John 4. In their desperation, these women sometimes go to church to be consoled. At church, a Korean male minister who thinks of himself as a servant of God tells them a typical male-centered interpretation of the Samaritan woman's story. According to this interpretation, she was a sinful woman because she had many husbands, yet nevertheless she could not be satisfied until she came to meet Jesus at a well and at last found a real and eternal life by drinking the living water offered by Jesus. Though the Samaritan woman is regarded as an immoral and sinful woman, these women are forced to identify themselves with her, and neither the Samaritan woman nor the present-day Korean women are given a chance to explain why they had to marry many times. Then, some of the present-day women come to confess that they are blessed to marry American GIs, for otherwise they could not have met Jesus. At the same time, they develop an antagonism against their country and people, both because they are betrayed or insulted by their people, and because they feel inferior on account of their shameful inter-marriage.

CONCLUSION

In the experience of Korean women, by drawing the parallel with the Samaritan woman, I could see how invasion by a foreign power is directly connected with a sexual invasion of the native women. These women's situations make it clear that the cause of the victimization of Korean women during the colonial periods is not monolithic at all, but proceeds from the multiple causes endemic to patriarchal imperialism. Their control over their own bodies and sexual functions was denied during the colonial periods. Yet, as Mineka Schipper correctly points out, once independence was achieved, and the war was over, people preferred to return to a so-called normal life where men's double standard functions well, regardless of how women had contributed or were victimized for the sake of the well-being of their country (10). As a result of this, the male double standard has rewarded these women with a "triple jeopardy." They are accused of betraying men, their country, and themselves, in that some of them respond to their victimization by becoming man-haters, while others are forced to turn their backs on their country in order to defend their marriage life, and still others betray their identity as women by utter dependence on their husbands (Minh-ha: 104). To make matters worse, the women who followed their American GI husbands to America have been further deprived of their ethnic or cultural identity by racism and Western cultural imperialism.

Thus, just as the voiceless Samaritan woman has been stereotyped as an immoral woman in the text, these women have had to endure their suffering life without any individual voice, but with a passive acceptance of life as an unavoidable destiny. But at least now we know the cause of their misery, and how Christianity also has marginalized their existence just by regarding them as the abandoned. As witnesses to the largely male victimization of women throughout human history, we no longer say that Korean women during the colonial periods, who were forced to identify themselves with the Samaritan woman, were sinful or immoral women. Furthermore, we are no longer deluded by the unchallenged authority of the Bible and of the Western church tradition which has not considered the voice of the marginalized in the biblical text as well as in present-day contexts, but which has aggravated the oppressive situation of these women. As a conclusion to this paper, therefore, I dare to suggest an ethical reading of John 4 through which the suffering but voiceless crying of Korean women during colonial periods can not only free the Samaritan woman who was falsely captured as an immoral woman in the text for 2,000 years, but can also awaken the privileged to see their own prejudice against these victimized women. In this way, the Samaritan woman's story cannot be told as an example of mission, or of the conversion of an immoral person, but as a prophetic voice of victimized women against imperialism.

WORKS CONSULTED

Botha, J. Eugene
    1991   *Jesus and the Samaritan Woman: A Speech Act Reading of John 4:1–42.*
              Leiden and New York: E. J. Brill.

Brown, Raymond E.
    1966   *The Gospel according to John.* New York: Doubleday.

Brownmiller, Susan
    1975   *Against Our Will: Men, Women and Rape.* New York: Simon & Schuster.

Carmichael, Calum M.
    1980   "Marriage and the Samaritan Woman." *NTS* 26:332–46.

Han, Kuk Yum
    1991   "Sexual Discrimination in Korean History." *Kidockgyosasang* 35:67–79.

Hicks, George
    1995   *The Comfort Women: Japan's Brutal Regime of Enforced Prostitution in the
              Second World War.* New York: W. W. Norton.

Hogan, M. P.
1976   "The Woman at the Well (John 4:1–42)." *TBT* 82:663–69.

Koester, Craig R.
1990   "The Savior of the World (John 4:42)." *JBL* 109:667–80.

1995   *Symbolism in the Fourth Gospel: Meaning, Mystery, Community.* Minneapolis: Fortress.

Mananzan, Mary John and Sun Ai Park
1986   "Emerging Spirituality of Asian Women." Pp. 77–88 in *With Passion and Compassion.* Ed. V. Fabella and M. A. Oduyoye. Maryknoll, NY: Orbis.

O'Day, Gail R.
1986   *Revelation in the Fourth Gospel.* Philadelphia: Fortress.

1992   "John." Pp. 293–304 in *The Women's Bible Commentary.* Ed. Carol A. Newsom and Sharon H. Ringe. Louisville: Westminster John Knox.

Olsson, Birger
1974   *Structure and Meaning in the Fourth Gospel: A Text-Linguistic Analysis of John 2:1–11 and 4:1–42.* Trans. J. Gray. ConBNT 6. Lund: C. W. K. Gleerup.

Park, Young Sook
1991   "Justice, Peace, and the Integrity of Creation." *In God's Image* 10:41–49.

Rodriguez, José David
1991   "The Challenge of Hispanic Ministry (Reflections on John 4)." *CurTM* 18:420–26.

Schipper, Mineka
1984   *Unheard Words: Women and Literature in Africa, the Arab World, Asia, the Caribbean and Latin America.* London: Allison & Busby.

Schneiders, Sondra M.
1989   "Women in the Fourth Gospel and the Role of Women in the Contemporary Church." *BTB* 12:35–45.

Trinh, Thi Min-ha
1989   *Women, Native, Other.* Bloomington and Indianapolis: Indiana University Press.

THE TRANSFORMATIVE POTENTIAL OF EPHESIANS IN A SITUATION OF TRANSITION

Elna Mouton
University of Port Elizabeth

ABSTRACT

The transformative potential of textual communication comes to the fore in an author's methods of persuasion and the implied response of her/his audience. The transformative power of the epistle to the Ephesians as ancient canonized text lies in its ability to disclose an alternative moral world, a new perspective on reality, albeit embedded within a patriarchal value system. The letter reflects a situation of transition characterized by a number of implied shifts in the orientation (vision of humanity) and language of its readers. With references to the metaphorical "world" of Christ's paradoxical example, the author emphasizes collective memory as a major recycling strategy towards the development of the community's moral identity and ethos, with healing and wholeness as major substance of their present and future hope. The structure of the rhetoric of Ephesians demonstrates an ongoing movement between orientation, disorientation, and reorientation. By means of the anthropological concept of liminality, the dynamics of the creative yet risky space between remembrance and hope presents a potential context for moral (trans)formation, with special reference to the South African situation of transition and its implications for women.

INTRODUCTION

The challenge of this essay is the continuing relevance or transformative potential of the biblical documents as ancient canonized texts originating from within patriarchal value systems. The epistle to the Ephesians provides a case study for describing the processes involved in textual communication. Its distinctiveness for this purpose is related to its explicit focus on the reinterpretation of power and its exigence of a deeply divided society as a possible analogy for the challenges facing South African churches at the moment. The kaleidoscope of cultural systems represented in the country are all intrinsically characterized by values such as patriarchy, gender and racial stereotyping, and social stratification, which necessarily obscure respect for human dignity in general, and the role and talent of women and their participation in social institutions in particular. These values profoundly determine the economic, political, relational, mechanical, and electronic "powers and principalities" in the market place, thereby influencing the quality of millions of people's lives. Moreover, our society is tortured by an exceptionally high incidence of power-related crimes such as murder and rape. The situation urgently challenges the integrity and relevance not only of the churches in South Africa, but also of theological education at large. It emphasizes the continuing need for the formation of moral agency, the empowerment of Christian identity and ethos, and an accountable use of Scripture in Christian ethos. The former often still functions as a justification of the "submissive" role of women in church and society.

Categories and skills developed by such related disciplines as anthropology, sociology, literary science, classical and modern rhetoric, and hermeneutics, support an examination of communication processes represented and stimulated by the Ephesian text. Its implied readers clearly find themselves within a liminal or transitional phase characterized by an encompassing change in the attitude of its readers' minds (4:23) marked by shifts both from a view of humanity defined by exclusivity and separation (between people and God and between Jewish and Gentile believers) to an identity and ethos of inclusivity and unity, and from an emphasis on cultic activities (covenant, circumcision, law, temple) to an emphasis on relations in which people of different ethnic groups, gender, and social status have been united with Christ into one body or household. As the medium between radically contrasting elements, between two different modes of existence, Ephesians functions as a threshold, a bridge, or a metaphor between the known and the unknown, between the "already" and the "not yet," and between remembrance and hope. It is particularly the dynamics of this "betwixt-and-between" stage that provides its author and readers with the stimulus, values, and virtues to redefine their humanity and moral existence. The author facilitates these processes by utilizing metaphor and tradition as rhetorical strategies. These seem to have a paraenetic and transformative function analogous to that of ritual and rites of passage during liminal phases in the lives of individuals and groups, reflected in liturgical elements such as prayer, hymns, and references to the initiating rite of baptism in 4:5; 5:26–27 (Kirby).

FROM BOUNDARIES TO THRESHOLDS: THE DYNAMICS OF LIMINALITY AS RECONCILIATORY STRATEGY BETWEEN DIFFERENT WORLDS

The concept of "liminality" was introduced by the French anthropologist Arnold van Gennep, who uses the term "rites of passage" in connection with the ceremonies and rituals performed at different stages in the life cycle of individuals and groups (birth, puberty, marriage, parenthood, retirement, and death). Van Gennep compares such events to the crossing of boundaries between territories. Like geographical boundaries that consist of stretches of land that function as neutral zones, a change from one phase of the life cycle to another often consists of a period of time that functions as a neutral zone, where the person is neither in the one stage nor in the other. These rites or ceremonies serve principally to provide guidance for the responsibilities encountered in the new phase (Van Gennep: 1–13, 21). Van Gennep distinguishes three types of rites, namely rites of separation from a previous world, rites of transition, and rites of incorporation into a new world (15–25, 192–94). Using the Latin word *limen* (threshold), he respectively calls these rites preliminal, liminal, and postliminal.

In the fields of cultural anthropology and sociology, the notion of liminality has since been developed further by several scholars, in particular by North American anthropologist Victor Turner. It has also been adapted and appropriated by theologians such as Gerald Arbuckle and Leo Perdue, both with reference to Turner, and Mark Kline (now McClain) Taylor (199–208), with reference to anthropologist Paul Rabinow. Mindful of the resocialization of Christian communities into new roles and groups, Arbuckle (31–37) reworked Turner's social-anthropological model (Turner: 37–42; Perdue: 9–11) by emphasizing three major phases during a time of change. The first involves a breach or separation from the known (often a well-structured, prosperous and orderly situation, also known as a *societas* phase). The second is a liminal, often a crisis phase of transition, during which previous roles, regulations, structures and certainties may be relativized and fundamentally rearranged. This phase is often a lengthy and complicated process, during which people feel an urgent need to discover meaning in what is happening, and to redefine their humanity. Turner (45–57, 273–74) refers to this as a *communitas* phase, a phase of "reflexivity" and "redressive action." A third phase is that of reintegration and reconstitution into new roles and groups, often by means of insights gained during the liminal phase. Taylor develops liminality, together with "admiration," as a Christian reconciliatory strategy for dealing with human differences. He observes, *"Liminality* is the term I reserve for the kind of life known 'betwixt and between' differentiated persons, groups or worlds. This is an experience of the wonder, the disorientation and discomfort that can rise when one is suspended between or among different groups or persons" (200).

Taylor describes the liminal space between cultural boundaries as a difficult, fragile, risky, and trying experience, of which the ambiguities and strains are not easily tolerated. At the same time the liminal encounter represents a dynamic and dialectic process wherein no one remains static. As new alliances are constructed in the interaction between different worlds, people's moral identities and lifestyles are reconstituted by it. Despite their different time-frames and historical situations, and the different disciplines from which they write, both Van Gennep and Taylor emphasize the elements of risk and creativity extant within liminality.

The addressees of the epistle to the Ephesians are referred to as "saints . . . the faithful in Christ Jesus" (1:1, 15). They seem mainly to originate from a Gentile background (2:11). The document presents its readers' movement and growth from one world to another, from a position outside Christ to being "in Christ," as a continuous wrestling to understand, a risky process with significant analogies to Van Gennep's stages of separation, transition, and incorporation. However, the structure of the Ephesian rhetoric does not seem necessarily to resemble a linear pattern guiding its readers from a preliminary into a postliminal phase, but rather a cyclical movement of continuous reinterpretation and renewal within liminal space. Its implied readers have already accepted Christ, and the author wishes to guide them towards a better understanding of that honorable position. He therefore does not introduce a movement into or out of liminality, but within liminality that he simply presupposes. The structure of this movement is a continual recycling of their life and world view—an ongoing reinterpretation of traditions, language, and behaviour in terms of Jesus Christ. By inducing a process of continuous reorientation to Christ, Ephesians serves as a warning against any form of moral stagnation, false stability, absolute certainty, or closed ethical system. It is in this context that I believe its rhetoric and quest for moral identity and appropriate behaviour has to be understood (1:4; 4:13; 5:27). In tandem with other disciplines, Van Gennep and Turner's analysis seem to be helpful in understanding the complex nature of liminality in a more nuanced way. In textual communication the movement within liminal space may be described in terms of the typical metaphorical processes of orientation, disorientation (alienation) and reorientation (Ricoeur, 1977; and McFague, among others).

BOUNDARIES AND IMPLIED SHIFTS IN THE MORAL IDENTITY AND ETHOS OF THE EPHESIAN COMMUNITY

Ephesians is generally divided into four major sections, namely the opening (1:1–2), a first and second main section (1:3–3:21 and 4:1–6:20, respectively), and the ending (6:21–24; see Mouton 1994:363–68; 1995:54–89). Both the greetings at the beginning and the farewell wishes at the end contain the powerful blessing of χάρις and εἰρήνη, summarizing the document's view on humanity as one of wholeness in relation to God and fellow-believers (1:6–7; 2:5–8, 14–17; 3:2, 7–8; 4:3; 6:15).[1] The eulogy of Eph 1:3–14 (with the significant recurrence of εὐλογεω in 1:3) announces the thrust of the first main section—and also of the whole document—as a celebration of God's gracious blessings toward all people in Christ. That section contains various elements

---

[1] Greek references in this essay are to the third edition of the Greek New Testament of the United Bible Societies (1975), and English references to the New International Version of the Bible (1989).

such as utterances of praise, thanksgiving, intercessory prayers and confessions of faith. It is generally accepted that all these elements express the doxological exclamation or appeal to praise God, followed by the reasons why God has to be praised, that are related to the typical Jewish prayer form called the *berakah* (Roberts: 15; Schnackenburg: 45–47). Fundamentally, the *berakah* was an act of remembrance or orientation, where God was to be praised for the way God had worked in the past. By remembering God's deeds, the people were moved again to praise God (Johnson: 58–59). In the case of Ephesians the act of remembering at the same time became an act of "dismembering" or disorientation—a typical trait of liminality—because of the way in which previous traditions such as election, covenant, law, and the temple with its dividing wall had to be reinterpreted in the light of the Christ event (1:4; 2:11–18; 4:7–10).

These details point to a possible historical situation for Ephesians in the prejudice and underlying tension between the Jewish and Gentile Christian communities in western Asia Minor during the first century CE (Eph 2:1). Whether the document dates from an early period such as 58–61 CE (Barth: 10–12; Roberts: 13), or a deutero-Pauline period (Sampley: 102; Schnackenburg: 24–29; Lincoln: xxxv–lxxiii), the basic "exigence" (Bitzer: 6) in terms of the struggle for identity among Jewish and Gentile Christians remained acute and was intensified after the Roman-Jewish War (66–70 CE,) when the tension between Jews and Christians gradually led to a break between the synagogue and the Christian communities around 85 CE. The thrust of Ephesians thus reveals a serious flaw in the implied readers' self-understanding. However, although the relation between Jewish and Gentile Christians seems to be the main need which the author wished to address, there were apparently also other even more basic features that distorted the Ephesian community's sense of humanity (for example, the inherently patriarchal structure seen in the household code in 5:21–6:9). Taylor argues, "The most fundamental form of otherness is male/female otherness. If this otherness is marked by opposition and disdain, it will be easier to oppose other others— be they black, Jewish, foreign, or poor." Only after reflection on this form of dominance has been done may exploration of the whole tangle of oppressions' infrastructure begin. From a contemporary perspective, one could therefore say that a complex set of issues probably contributed to the exigence behind Ephesians, namely, the confirmation of the readers' identity and ethos in relation to Christ and one another. Within this context the power of Christ's sacrificial love is emphasized as a reconciliatory strategy through which any "dividing wall" between people had been abolished.

Another significant trait of the first main section is that its different elements are arranged in an a-b-c-b-a chiastic pattern. This means that not only the recurring elements of the eulogy in 1:3–14 and the doxology in 3:20–21, and the two intercessory prayers in 1:15–21 and 3:1, 14–19 are emphasized by the particular structure, but specifically the confession of faith in 1:22–23 (with its three illustrative explanations in 2:1–22) as a non-repeating middle section (Roberts: 14–19). The dramatic consequences of 1:22–23 are particularly described in transitional terms: Those who were dead, have been made alive (2:1–10); those who were far away, excluded from citizenship in Israel, have been brought near (2:11–18); and those who formerly had been powerless and statusless foreigners and aliens (ξένοι καὶ πάροικοι), have been made fellow-citizens with God's people and members of God's household (2:19–22). By destroying the barrier of hostility through his cross (2:14–16), Christ gave birth to a new creation, a new humanity.

The pivotal confession of 1:22–23, which summarizes the preceding prayer (1:12–21), deals with two closely related matters: the exalted position of Jesus as resurrected and sovereign lord, and his significance as a gift of salvation to the believers as liminals. The second aspect defines the first in a profound and surprising way. In the context of Ephesians, Christ's magnificent power and honor (as lord and head) is decisively yet paradoxically defined in terms of his sacrificial love, humility and care as servant (1:7; 2:13, 16; 4:32; 5:2, 25, 29). This position is characterized particularly by the memory of his cross—the rite of passage *par excellence*, which he performed on behalf of his followers. His cross, resurrection, and ascension guaranteed their salvation through faith in him, and yet would throw them into a permanent state of liminality. The metaphors of head, body, and fullness thus function as shifting devices in thrusting the readers' thoughts towards a full understanding of their new humanity in Christ (Cloete and Smit).

Two factors accomplish this linking of the experience of Christ to the identity of the believers in their situation of liminality. First, the images of head (1:10; 4:15–16; 5:23, 29–30), body (4:12–16; 5:29–30), and fullness (3:19; 4:13; 5:18) in 1:22–23 stress the close and inseparable relationship between God's people and Christ. As head, Christ incorporated all who belong to him into one body when he accomplished their salvation. What has happened to him has happened to them. When he was raised from the dead, they were raised with him. When he was seated at God's right hand, they were seated with him (2:4–6). The structure of 2:6 is syntactically parallel to that of 1:20, which is of major rhetorical significance (note the two aorist indicatives συνήγειρεν and συνεκάθισεν in 2:6, and the two aorist participles ἐγείρας and καθίσας in 1:20. The second factor is the symbol of the cross. Within the Mediterranean sociological world of the first century, death on a cross was considered as an extremely shameful event (Olyan: 214 n. 43). In Ephesians this symbol is reinterpreted and becomes, through the resurrection, an honorable deed for the benefit of those who adhere to him by faith (Meeks, 1993:14–15, 61–65, 131–35). It is the memory of these glorious yet strange events that was meant to shape the moral identity and ethos of the readers of Ephesians during the liminal process.

The second main section of the letter consists primarily of paraenetic elements directed to the church. These are interwoven with theological and christological motivations, and intrinsically linked to and informed by the first main section. The structural and semantic coherence between the two main sections is indicated by such conjunctions as οὖν, τουτο οὖν and διο in 4:1, 17, 25 and 5:15, which indicate the particular sections they introduce as a direct and logical consequence of what had been said before (Mouton, 1995:71–76; Hendrix). The essence of Ephesians 1–3 (a new humanity in relation to Christ and fellow-believers) is thus explicated in terms of a life worthy of their calling (4:1). In fact, it was particularly the *communitas* experience of reconciliation between Jewish and Gentile Christians that opened their eyes to recognize their full potential in Christ. Ephesians 4–6 contain the radical implications of this insight. They should be "kind and compassionate to one another, forgiving each other, just as in Christ God forgave you" (4:32). They should live a life of love, "just as Christ loves you and gave himself up for you" (5:2; 4:2). They were to "put on the new self, created to be like God in true righteousness and holiness" (4:24). Within the covenant vocabulary of the Hebrew Bible, honor was closely connected with justice, righteousness, and peace (Olyan: 202 n. 3). Consequently, the virtues and values characteristic of their new paradoxical status in Christ were also meant to redefine the traditionally patriarchal relations described in the domestic code of 5:21–6:9. The husband, for instance, hears that he is the head of the wife "as Christ is the head of the church" (5:23). Christ's headship is characterized by the power of his love—a power which is paradoxically revealed in the "weakness" of his suffering. The husband also has to submit to his wife (5:21), and to love her "just as Christ loved the church and gave himself up for her" (5:25). The domestic code likewise encourages the wife to claim her primary identity in Christ and to be empowered by his example. Her role implies submission to a husband whose humanity is implicitly modelled on the example of Christ.

THE STRUCTURE OF THE EPHESIAN RHETORIC AS AN ONGOING MOVEMENT WITHIN LIMINAL SPACE

The continuing, risky process by which the Ephesian readers had to learn to match their new identity to a lifestyle (and language) worthy of their calling, occurred in the creative, liminal tension between remembrance and hope. While remembering not only their former way of living as Gentiles (2:11, 12), but especially what God has done for them in Christ (1:3–3:20; 4:20–24; 5:8), they were looking forward to the "day of redemption" when they would inherit their full salvation (1:14; 4:30). In the interim their hope would be kept alive by their memory of the Christ event and through their response to the ongoing encounter with the risen Christ and the Spirit (2:22;

3:17; 4:6, 10, 30; 5:18). Amid the danger of evil powers (6:10–13), it was particularly from within the liminal space that they would be transformed and energized to grow toward their full potential in Christ (4:1, 12–16; 5:23–24, 32; 5:1–2; 6:10).

The Ephesian author facilitates this process by continuously reminding his readers of the privilege and associated ethos of their new position in Christ, in contrast to who they were before. In this way he maintains the cyclical movement within their liminal situation. Significant in this regard is the present imperative μνημονεύετε introducing 2:11–19 ("Remember that formerly you who are Gentiles by birth . . . were separate from Christ, excluded from citizenship in Israel and foreigners to the covenants of the promise . . . But now in Christ Jesus you . . . have been brought near"). It denotes a continuous redeeming of the past, while confirming the readers' new beginning in Christ (Lategan, 1996:229).

The cyclical structure of the rhetoric in the intercessory prayer of 1: 15–23 is emphasized by the author's introduction in 1:16–18. The main verb οὐ παύομαι is followed by two present participles (εὐχαριστῶν ὑπὲρ ὑμῶν and μνείαν ποιούμενος), as well as a purpose clause in the perfect tense (εἰς τὸ εἰδέναι ὑμᾶς), implying a continuous effect in the present ("I have not stopped giving thanks for you, remembering you in my prayers. I keep asking the God of our Lord Jesus Christ . . . that you may know . . ."). The rest of the first main section pictures the grace of God—the basic motivation for the believers' new identity—in terms of a continuous present activity (1:19, 23; 2:4, 8, 10, 18–19, 21–22; 3:6, 12–13, 15, 20).

It is especially in the paraenetic section of Ephesians (chs. 4–6) that the cyclical pattern of its rhetoric comes to the fore. Within the broad structure of the document (Mouton, 1995:55–76), the present imperatives in 4:17, 23, 25, 30, 32; 5:1–2, 8b, 10, 18–21 (as well as other present tense forms in those two chapters) indicate a process of continuous moral formation in accordance with the community's new identity in Christ. The imperatives following 5:18 ("Be filled with the Spirit . . .") in the domestic code and the armor of God passage confirm the rhetorical pattern of continuous action in the present as the only proper ethos worthy of their calling (5:24–25, 27–29, 33; 6:1–10, 16, 18).

In this open-ended movement within liminality, the question may arise as to what extent the rhetoric of Ephesians allows for the existence or formation of boundaries. How, for instance, would a community of faith whose understanding of God and reality is characterized by a cyclical movement of reinterpretation deal with the continual confrontation with and assimilation of strangers, and with new knowledge, new experiences, and new situations? From within the context of Ephesians it is clear that any structures and boundaries (necessary though they may be under given circumstances) would only be justifiable in as far as they impel movement, communication, healing, reconciliation, and moral formation (Taylor: 207). Where they inhibit movement, stop communication, or absolutize differences, they have to be dismantled. The rhetorical processes in Ephesians resemble an ongoing interaction between the identity awareness and ethos of followers of Christ. The document thus considers the creativity, tension, paradox, and risk of liminal spaces as the optimal context for moral formation and growth.

Within the movement of the Ephesian rhetoric mentioned above, the nature of Christ's power in 1:22 and its relation to wifely submission in 5:22 deserve special attention. It is rhetorically significant that the strategic verb ὑποτάσσω in 1:22 (as part of the faith confession) recurs in its middle form (ὑποτάσσομαι) in the paraenetical section of the document (5:21, 24). In both instances it is surrounded and nuanced by a context referring to the fullness or wholeness of the body of Christ. The verb ὑποτάσσω, meaning to subject to or to bring under the control of someone (Louw and Nida: 476), was used as a military term in the first-century Mediterranean context, referring to the acknowledgment of a person's status, dignity, and authority embodied in others' obedience, loyalty, and submission to that person's directives and wishes (Louw and Nida: 468). The verb ὑποτάσσεται in 5:24 likewise means "to take a subordinate role in relation to that of another" (Lincoln: 367).

As a general injunction and motivation, respectively, Eph 5:21 and 6:9b frame the household code by reinterpreting its patriarchal structure from a christological perspective. Ephesians 5:21 is a transitional verse "completing the series of participles which are dependent on the verb πληροῦσθε, 'be filled,' from v. 18, while itself providing the verbal form on which the first injunction in the . . . household code is dependent" (Lincoln: 365). The idiomatic expression in 6:9b (καὶ προσωπολημψία οὐκ ἔστιν παρ᾽ αὐτῷ) literally means "He does not lay hold of someone's face"—in other words, "He does not esteem anyone according to face value," as in Deut 10:17; 16:19; Lev 19: 15; Matt 22:16; Mk 12:14; Lk 20:21; Acts 10:34; Rom 2:11; Gal 2:6; Col 3:25 (Louw and Nida: 768). It probably originated in the context of slavery, where slaves were chained to one another while waiting to be sold on the market. As inferiors they were not allowed to lift up their heads until a potential buyer would do so, sometimes brutally, in order to examine their teeth and general health. In Eph 6:9, as well as parallel expressions in Deut 10:17; 16: 19 and Lev 19:15, this phrase occurs in a context which emphasizes God's sovereignty and almighty power. In contrast to the often abusive power of contemporary authorities, the essence of God's power is defined in terms of loving care and concern for people, and particularly by God's restoring what was lost to them, namely, their dignity and humanity. The Ephesian author thus seems radically to reverse the patriarchal connotation of ὑποτάσσω (as imposed loyalty and obedience) to reflect not only the essence of the relationship between Christ and the church (in terms of willing honor and reverence), but also among the members of the body itself. On this point, note also the semantically related terms φοβέομι in 5:33, ὑπακούω in 6:1, 5, and τιμάω in 6:2, which all relate to the guiding principle for wise living in the Old Testament covenant, namely the "fear of Yнwн," which is reinterpreted here as the overriding motivation for wise Christian living (1:8, 17; 5:15) and for relationships within the new community. It is an attitude that looks to Christ in awe at his overwhelming love and power (Lincoln: 365–68). These expressions implicitly resemble the thrust of the document as a radical reinterpretation of human relations in the light of the Christ event.

However, read from a twentieth-century feminist perspective, and reading from within the current socio-political context in South Africa, the patriarchal language that expresses and constitutes the christologically reinterpreted notion of mutual submission in the domestic code (5:21) creates tension and a sense of inconsistency particularly with regard to the role of wives and slaves, and therefore runs a serious risk of being abused by later readers.

Nowhere in Ephesians is the vulnerability of the hermeneutical process better illustrated than by the relation between its liberating vision of reconciliation, unity, and mutuality, and the typical patriarchal language that describes that vision by notions such as "sonship" (1:15), Christ as "head" (1: 22; 4:15; 5:23), "one new man" (2:15), "wifely submission" (5:22), and slaves' obedience with "respect and fear" toward their masters (6:5). The paradigm used for Christian marriage in 5:22–33 is the relation between Christ and the church. Wives are made the image of the church, whereas husbands are made the image of Christ, which gives a theological basis to an inferiority of the female to the male in terms of a divinely willed order. In spite of the radical reinterpretation of patriarchal domination by the paradoxical example of Christ, Fiorenza argues that this theological paradigm

> reinforces the cultural-patriarchal pattern of subordination, insofar as the relationship between Christ and the church clearly is not a relationship between equals, since the church-bride is totally dependent and subject to her head or bridegroom. Therefore, the general injunction for all members of the Christian community, "Be subject to one another in the fear of Christ," is clearly spelled out for the Christian wife as requiring submission and inequality. (1983:269)

For Fiorenza, the christological modification of the husband's role "does not have the power, theologically, to transform the patriarchal pattern of the household code, even though this might have been the intention of the author. Instead, Ephesians christologically cements the inferior position of the wife in the marriage relationship." She concludes that the author was not able to Christianize the code: "The gospel of peace has transformed the relationship of gentiles and Jews, but not the social roles of wives and slaves within the household of God" (1983:270). It therefore seems that the radical and moral instruction of Jesus gradually was eroded by compromises with the dominant world view. The Ephesian text shows "a community experimenting, growing, wrestling and ultimately failing to embody the vision of its founder" (Draper: 50). Although the author of Ephesians does not seem to find these aspects incompatible (Lincoln: 366), the tension between the document's dynamic, complementary perspective and its hierarchical language may inhibit its transformative potential for later readers.

Although the constricting structures of patriarchy and slavery are not directly addressed in Ephesians, radically new values and attitudes are introduced—its radicality and newness being embodied in the example of Christ. Though it is even doubtful whether its intended effect made a dramatic difference in, for example, the subordinate role of women in the first centuries CE (Botha; Meeks, 1983:23–25; 1993:49–50, 138–47), it appears that the document was meant to reorient both Jews and gentiles, and both men and women, according to their previous social status of either power or powerlessness. How would such a process work epistemologically in terms of experience and explanation?

THE TRANSFORMATIVE POTENTIAL OF EPHESIANS: THE MORAL FUNCTION OF ITS RHETORICAL STRATEGIES

The (re)orienting potential of metaphor is an essential element of liminality and of the rhetorical and transformative aspects of Ephesians. Like rites of passage, the rhetorical strategies in Ephesians function to shape and to remind its readers of their identity and appropriate ethos during a time of fundamental change. In this context our interest in metaphors particularly lies in their referential (redescriptive) and relational nature (Lategan, 1985, 1994b, 1996:226–28; Van Huyssteen). Lategan rightly claims that a "better understanding of the function of reference in all its forms holds the key to unlock the transformative potential of (biblical) texts in contemporary situations" (1994b:34, 1996:229). According to Ricoeur (1975; 1976:89–95; 1977: 216–56), the referential or transformative power of a text lies in its ability to suggest, to open up, to facilitate, to mediate, to make possible, to produce a "world in front of it," a "proposed world" which readers may adopt or inhabit. In this way it discloses a possible new way of looking at things. The transformative potential of a text concurs with the notion of the implied reader as "a device to engage the real reader by offering a role to be played or an attitude to be assumed" (Lategan, 1989:10). It is "the reader we have to be willing to become in order to bring the reading experience to its full measure" (Vorster: 25).

Metaphor in particular can help people to integrate and to redescribe their experiences by changing the (meaning of the) language they use. Metaphors are heuristic devices for the redescription of reality or lived experience,

which break up inadequate interpretations of the world and open the way
to new, more adequate interpretations (Lategan, 1993:404–7; 1994a:21). By
means of comparison, a metaphor creates a relation of meaning between two
things in such a surprising way that something new comes to the fore about
the unknown factor in the comparison. It is especially this important observation that metaphors redescribe reality that brings about a better understanding of our knowledge and experience of reality (Ricoeur, 1976:45–69,
1977:239–46, 1980:25–27). Sallie McFague (14–29) deals with the interactional
and referential function of metaphor as an element basic to the understanding of human thinking and language in general, and the communicative
processes of reinterpretation and liminality in particular. As an act of remembrance and dismembrance, then, metaphor as well as story and tradition
as an extended metaphor becomes a crucial instrument for survival in the
liminal space—a possible way of decoding "the traces of God's presence in
history" (Ricoeur, 1980:26). For these reasons it has been suggested above
that the exigence or rhetorical situation presented by the Ephesian document
(the position from which the author wished to guide his readers' thoughts
and behavior through discourse) be investigated as an imperfection in the
readers' concept of humanity. To persuade gentile Christians of their equal
status with Jewish Christians, and wives and husbands, children and parents, slaves and masters of their mutuality in Christ, the author utilizes a
network of metaphors and traditions as metaphorical expressions.

   The Genre of Ephesians as Reinterpreted Tradition. The genre of the document functions metaphorically to affirm the readers' new identity and ethos.
According to Holland Hendrix the document's structure shows remarkable
parallels to the typical honorific decrees found on monuments and inscrip-
tions in Greco-Roman antiquity. In the moral world of first-century Asia
Minor, honors for benefactors were a well-known phenomenon:

> As with many decrees, Ephesians is a prescription of reality. The author
> adapts a pervasive social reality, the benefactor-beneficiary phenomenon,
> and through his adaptation prescribes a new network of benefaction. What
> is achieved is a powerful reinforcement of Christian identity and cohesion.
> Christians are those who honor their divine benefactor through moral be-
> havior, animated by love as expressed in mutual benefit. (Hendrix: 10)

The purpose of ancient honorific decrees was constantly to remind bene-
ficiaries of their inheritance and to persuade them towards specific action.
Hendrix emphasizes the ethos associated with a specific social identity and
again finds a striking parallel in Ephesians:

> An ethos of reciprocal benefactions and honor for the common good of the
> People and the glory of her patrons was the social premise of the benefactor-
> beneficiary phenomenon. It is precisely this ethos which is articulated in a
> "Christianized" form in Ephesians. As the ultimate benefactors, God and

Christ are honored through moral behavior that mutually benefits God's people. (Hendrix: 10)

Understanding the Ephesian document as a reinterpreted "honorific decree" embedded in the epistolary genre illuminates its overwhelming emphasis on Christ's lordship and the author's and recipients' exalted position of power (1:10, 19–23; 2:5, 6). This understanding also clarifies the document's alternative ethos of praise-giving (1:6, 12, 14; 3:20–21; 5:20), unity (4:1–16), and mutual submission (5:21) associated with those who believe that what God did was for their benefit (1:19; 5:25). Within the liminal phase of their "becoming," the author acts as mediator and reminder of the universal gifts of God's beneficence in Christ (1:3–14) and calls his readers to appropriate honor of God and mutual caring for one another (4:25–32; 5:1–21) as expressions of this "common good of the people and the glory of her patrons."

Temporal and Spatial Indicators. Functioning like metaphors, various persuasive techniques or *topoi* are embedded within the encompassing device of the Ephesian genre, by means of which the author wishes to shift his audience from one position to another. These refer to aspects of people, time, and place (Vorster, 1990:123). *Topoi* necessarily reflect the value system of a group or society, and can therefore not be separated from the socio-historical and moral world within which they function.

Deeply concerned about his audience's perception of their primary status "in Christ," the Ephesian author uses every possible means to contrast their previous (shameful, powerless) position and behavior with that of their present (honorable, powerful) situation and corresponding ethos. In different ways temporal and spatial indicators mark the decisive "before" and "after" of the readers' coming to faith (2:1–6, 11–13, 19–22; 4:17–24; 5:8). The period of their present status is seen as fundamentally different from their previous status. Their position of dishonor has been replaced by a position of honor. In contrast to a shameful and powerless position where they had been looked down upon by the Jews (2:11–13), excluded from citizenship in Israel and viewed as aliens to the covenant (2:12, 19), they are now depicted as fellow-citizens of God's people and members of God's household—a dwelling in which God lives by God's Spirit (2:22).

The temporal and spatial indicators in Ephesians function on two important levels. First, they are used to identify different dispensations and preferred or non-preferred positions. Second, they are used as a rhetorical strategy "to effect the shifting of position" (Lategan, 1993:402). Indicating preferred and non-preferred positions is one thing. To achieve a shift in the right direction is, however, quite another matter. How does the author go about ensuring the desired result? How does he influence his readers to accept their new, advantageous position, even after they have come to faith (1:1, 15)? How is their change of attitude and behavior supposed to take place?

For the Ephesian author the key to change is provided by the interrelated communication processes of orientation, disorientation, and reorientation (Ricoeur, 1975:122–28, 1976:46–53, 1977:65–100; McFague: 46–48), alienation and re-identification (Du Toit), association and disassociation (Lategan, 1993:402), or distanciation and appropriation (Hartin: 514–16). These processes essentially reveal the (re)orientating or transformative potential of metaphorical language, which forms the heart of (biblical) hermeneutics as a boundary-crossing subject.

The Persuading Potential of Jesus Christ as Metaphor. The Ephesian metaphors serve as windows through which the processes of identification, estrangement, and reorientation, typical of the image-making capacity of the human mind in a situation of liminality, can be viewed. Any creative act of interpretation, discovery, decision-making, transition, or transformation can be recognized as the imaginative combination and synthesis of the familiar into new wholes (McFague: 35–36), which is a redescription of reality (Ricoeur, 1975:122–28, 1976:45–69, 1980:26). With reference to McFague (31–66, 90–194), Christ's role in Ephesians may be described as an extended "metaphor or parable for God" and a "model for Christian behavior." These notions have the potential to impact on biblical readers (especially in times of *communitas*) by continuously reorienting and transforming their self-understanding and ethos as disciples of Jesus Christ. As with metaphors, the essence of parable is that it works by indirection, through the ordinary, mundane, and secular, to bring about new insight. This means that we start with the more familiar work of Jesus from "below," and move indirectly to his person, and to the invisible, unfamiliar God whom Jesus represents. The whole network of Jesus' life—his words and deeds and particularly his death, resurrection, and exaltation—thus provides a grid or screen through which the understanding of God can be realigned (McFague: 49–54; Hays, 1990:45–50).

How does Jesus' designation as parable of God realign, redefine, or reorient (Ricoeur, 1975:122–28, 1976:89–95, 1977:216–56) people's understanding of God? As a true and novel metaphor, Jesus as parable always reorders, shocks, and upsets familiar, conventional preconceptions and understandings of God. McFague believes that the heart of the drama of Jesus' life and death is the tension that it manifests between accepted ways of relating to God and to others and a new way of living in the world. As such, Jesus' life and especially his death and resurrection have to be viewed as radical and iconoclastic, continuously calling into question the comfortable and secure homes that our interpretations of God have built for us (McFague: 51–54). In this sense the church finds itself in a constant situation of liminality: Like Christ we are called to a life *in* but not *of* the world, and to lives that always stand in criticism of the status quo and that press toward fulfillment of the body of Christ.

The ultimate purpose of the Ephesian author's use of Christ as metaphor and parable is to provide a basis for the readers' new self-understanding and perspective on reality (Lategan, 1993:404–6). A major strategy he uses in accomplishing this is to emphasise his own and the readers' identification with Christ. He reminds them that their own dramatic change was not self-initiated, but rather was effected by the closest possible association with Christ, in his death and resurrection, and especially in his exaltation to the right hand of God (1:18–21; Lincoln: 61). "Change cannot be achieved on one's own or in isolation—only in solidarity with Christ and with fellow-believers" (Lategan, 1993:405). In this way Christ functions not only as a parable, but also as a model inducing specific behavior. This means that specific virtues and values associated with him are generated toward those who identify with him. In the context of Ephesians these include humility, love, forgiveness, righteousness, peace, and hope.

Through various strategies the Ephesian author encourages his readers to think of themselves in terms of the new position they ought to assume—as fellow-citizens with God's people, as one body in Christ, as a new humanity. The preferred position indicated by persuasive strategies in the document is the continuous renewal of their spirit and ethos in accordance with God's righteousness and holiness (4:23–24). By inviting humankind to assume its honorable status in Christ, Ephesians offers its readers a new self-understanding, leading to a new ethos, new attitudes and actions. To summarize, one may say that the starting point of all persuasive strategies is the delicate, liminal tension between identification, alienation, and reorientation. For later readers these processes hold the key to the transformative potential of the biblical documents. To inhabit their strange, alternative world is not only a gift of God's grace (Eph 2:5, 8–10), but also a faithful hermeneutical choice: "In a co-operative shared work, the Spirit, the text, and the reader engage in a transforming process, which enlarges horizons and creates new horizons" (Thiselton: 619).

REVISIONING THE LIMINAL ENCOUNTER BETWEEN EPHESIANS AND CONTEMPORARY READERS

It has become clear that the Ephesian epistle is characterized by the dynamic, liminal process of the early Christian communities' search to understand human existence in the light of the Christ event (Meeks, 1993:1–17, 109–10). The unique hallmark of this process is their continuous and radical reorientation to the alien, completely other, yet for them truthful story of Jesus Christ. However, the document's christological-ecclesial perspective does not only orient the interpretive processes implied by the text itself, but implicitly also those activated and facilitated by it (Verhey: 179–87). An ethically responsible reading of Ephesians by subsequent readers thus calls for a

continuous wrestling, for imaginative, Spirit-filled, and critical reflection
on the active presence and will of God in ever changing times and circumstances. The processes and obstacles involved in such a journey are implied
and anticipated in the Ephesian text itself. Amid its glorious "in Christ"
vision and powerful human potential for the good, it also reckons with the
fragile realities of human cultural limitations and fallibility and its inclina-
tion to evil impulses. This gives pause to all hopes that character and virtue
can be created instantly so as to guarantee good. However, Ephesians assures
its readers that they are not left alone in their struggle for the good. Rather,
God provides Christ and his body as the full armor of his protection against
the powers and principalities, the spiritual forces of evil in the heavenly
realms (Eph 6:10–20). The memory of Christ's story, and of the faith community's story in the light of it, is meant to remain a source of living hope in the
present. In this way liminality may lead to deepened faith experiences and
reflection on God. For this reason professional and ordinary readers of the
Bible share the moral obligation to engage in the creative tension of the liminal space between the dynamics of the biblical texts and the multiple needs,
fears, dreams, and hopes of contemporary readers (Fiorenza, 1988:13).

The question is how the culturally-bound alternative world of Ephesians
may be brought into relation with, and impact on, present-day moral challenges. In accordance with its relational nature, the authority of Ephesians
for subsequent readers first of all resides in the continuing encounter with
the living God mediated and stimulated by the text (Lategan, 1992:154,
1994a:131–33). The transformative potential of Ephesians lies in its referential
power, in its ability to point beyond itself to a reality which it could only describe in a limited and provisional manner, namely, the full story of Christ.
The Ephesian vision of humanity invites its later readers to commemorate
this story liturgically and practically, with awe and admiration.

To respond faithfully and with sensitivity to the rhetorical function
of Ephesians is to account for its transformative potential amid its cultural-
historical biases—that is, the typically human process of redescription in
the light of new knowledge and experience underlying it. Involvement in
the liminal space therefore asks for an open-endedness which humbly recognizes the provisional nature of all faith utterances. To allow for explanations
and experiences of a living God who is constantly revealed in new and surprising ways (Hays: 32–33; Meeks, 1993:217–19), later readers of Ephesians
are challenged to account for its patriarchal language, and to create the
inclusive language needed to express and construct their experiences. The
document does not bind us in a rigid, legalistic way, but liberates us towards
the imaginative appropriation of the mighty, healing power of God's love in
new circumstances. In spite of its patriarchal embeddedness, the document
invites contemporary readers to identify with Christ in the paradoxical tri-
umph of his resurrection and exaltation and to grow beyond all limited and

stereotypical views of humanity. We have seen how the dynamics of liminality function in Ephesians as a reconciliatory strategy between different moral worlds, providing for its readers the vision, values, and skills to redefine their humanity. Therefore, to respect its transformative potential is to dedicate oneself to accomplishing the full potential of the body of Christ. Anything less would confine the God of Ephesians to the boundaries of an ancient canonised text in a way contradictory to its own nature, and can therefore not be considered as normative.

For me as a white South African woman from within the Reformed tradition, this poses a formidable challenge. Reading Ephesians has become a liberating and frightening experience to me. Liberating, because of the Christian story's potential to enable all people to become mature persons in Christ, yet also frightening because of the power of our ideologically-based interpretive frameworks and presuppositions, and the reality of our moral world which in many, many respects seems to be so far away from this vision. At the moment our society is undergoing a very rapid transition from what may broadly be described as a (homogeneous) premodern to a (pluralistic) modern and even postmodern phase (Smit: 20–21). The evil spirit of apartheid (including sexism, racism, and classism), a "dividing wall of hostility" (Eph 2:14; 6:12), has deeply distorted the sense of humanity and identity of all people in South Africa in every possible way. No one is unaffected by it, even those who do not realize it: the poor and the rich, women and men, black and white. Tragically, we all carry personal scars and the scars of our country's history.

· In the transformational process in South Africa, since April 1994, racial oppression has understandably been prioritized as the primary sin to be eradicated. However, "the instructured mechanisms of race, gender and class in the oppression of people have not been adequately understood" (Ackermann, 1994:201). Although the interim and new South African constitutions (the latter promulgated in December of 1996) guarantee gender equality, and in spite of the South African Reconstruction and Development Programme's key focus on ensuring an equal role for women in every aspect of the economy and society, the international agency Human Rights Watch found that South African women remain second class citizens (Friedman). The report tells of an extraordinarily high incidence of abuse, discrimination, and violence against women in this country. Ackermann substantiates this statement with reference to a 1993 local newspaper report: "In Berlin, delegates to the ninth International Conference on AIDS were told that in South Africa at least one woman is raped every 83 seconds, and 95 per cent of rape victims are black" (1994:206). Statistics for 1996 indicate that rape now occurs in South Africa every eighteen seconds!

The major crisis arising from this situation for me, however, is the silence of many churches on these issues:

138   SEMEIA

An appalling and too often unacknowledged side of the endemic violence in
our society is the sexual violence inflicted on women and children. Even if
this fact is acknowledged, it is often not understood that sexual violence is
essentially an evil abuse of power. As such, it is a theological problem.
Racism and sexism are structures of domination which create conditions for
the abuse of power . . . A number of churches and certain church leaders
have been justly vocal in their condemnation of apartheid. Few, if any, have
spoken out against sexism. (Ackermann, 1994:205)

There have been significant changes. However, the memory of nearly two
thousand years of a male-dominated church, backed by theology that is derived from mainly western male scholarship, has left us with an enormous
challenge. The most serious part of this heritage, is its implicit and explicit
theological justification. As in the case of Eph 5:22, the patriarchal language
of the biblical documents often still serves to legitimate the secondary role of
women in the home, church, and society. Even more acute is the theological
problem which is created when humanity and the nature of God are pre-
dominantly represented in terms of male images.

To deal with the situation creatively, I wish to propose a "hermeneutic of
liminality" that reclaims the transformative potential of the biblical writings
as an invitation to accomplish a healed and full body of Christ. "Transformative potential" here refers to the search for a communal and ecumenical
justice, not in an absolutistic way the justice of a particular interest group,
necessary though that may be under given circumstances. In the context
of this essay, "transformative potential" is therefore to be regarded as post-
feminist and post-liberal. In terms of the Ephesian perspective, such a vision invites Christians to develop what H. Richard Niebuhr calls a "common
memory," in which persons not only share the present life, but also adopt
as their own the past history of others. "Where common memory is lacking,
where men (sic) do not share in the same past, there can be no real community, and where community is to be formed common memory must be
created" (86). This means that we will have to be open to listen to the stories
of all the people in South Africa, particularly those who have not been considered as important in the past, and to adopt the past—including the past
sins—of other groups as our own, and to risk to forgive them and ourselves
for what we have done to each other. This will allow us the opportunity to
lament the loss of our full humanity for such a long time, and to grow from
remembering our inherited traditions of alienation to *dismembering* them in the
light of Christ's healing love. In this sense the present liminal context may
be conducive to understanding Christ's inclusive and relational view of humanity in a new way. It will hopefully become a *kairos* moment, a rebirth, a
resurrection in terms of rethinking and redefining our humanity. In concur-
rence with Ackermann's relational anthropology (1991:100–103; 1992:16–23)
and feminist theology as liberating praxis (1994:201–8), the key words in a

hermeneutic of liminality are "relationality" and "risk." "Relationality as basis for a transformative view of humanity is . . . concerned with our relationships with ourselves, with one another, with God and with our environment" (Ackermann, 1991:102). It is the opposite of alienation, apathy, and exclusion. "Risk" refers to the courage, energy, and commitment required to deal with the deeply entrenched power of patriarchy and other forms of oppression (Ackermann, 1994:207). Christ is our model with regard to this stereoscopic vision of transformation. Ephesians witnesses that Christ is able to translate different stories into one new story (1:10), into a new common memory, which might become a common hope for the future. In terms of Taylor's vision of a "postmodern trilemma" (40–45), it challenges us to respect, and where necessary creatively to reinterpret, tradition, to celebrate plurality, and to resist any form of domination.

A hermeneutic of liminality does not allow for final, unalterable answers, decisions, and certainties. It rather challenges us to live patiently and humbly with the tension of risk (the risk to remember, to love, to forgive, to hope), the tension of paradox, ambivalence, pain, and even ridicule. Appropriating the perspective of Ephesians in terms of the formation of moral people, the transformation of a moral society, and the information of moral action is a slow, lifelong, more often than not cumbersome process. It nevertheless continues to encourage followers of Christ towards the realization of the full potential of his body. There is no instant way toward accomplishing it. It is a narrow road which calls for a hermeneutic of trust, hope, and commitment.[2]

WORKS CONSULTED

Ackermann, Denise
1991   "Being Woman, Being Human." Pp. 93–105 in *Women Hold Up Half the Sky: Women in the Church in Southern Africa.* Ed. Denise Ackermann, Jonathan A. Draper, and Emma Mashinini. Pietermaritzburg: Cluster.

1992   "Defining Our Humanity: Thoughts on a Feminist Anthropology." *JTSA* 79:13–23.

1994   "Faith and Feminism: Women Doing Theology." Pp. 197–211 in *Doing Theology in Context: South African Perspectives.* Ed. John De Gruchy and Charles Villa-Vicencio. Maryknoll: Orbis.

2 My sincere thanks goes to my colleagues Helena Glanville and Helen Efthimiadis, as well as to Dr. Vernon Robbins of Emory University for fruitful discussions on the subject, and for their helpful comments on previous drafts of the essay.

Arbuckle, Gerald A.
1991   *Grieving for Change: A Spirituality for Refounding Gospel Communities.*
        London: Geoffrey Chapman.

Barth, Markus
1974   *Ephesians 1–3.* New York: Doubleday.

Bitzer, Lloyd F.
1968   "The Rhetorical Situation." *Philosophy and Rhetoric* 1:1–14.

Botha, Pieter J. J.
1992   "Folklore, Social Values and Life as a Woman in Early Christianity."
        S. A. Journal for Folklore Studies 3:1–14.

Cloete, G. Daan and Dirk J. Smit
1988   "Preaching from the Lectionary: Eph 1:20–23." *JTSA* 63:59–67.

Domeris, William R.
1993   "Honour and Shame in the New Testament." *Neot* 27:283–97.

Draper, Jonathan A.
1991   "Oppressive and Subversive Moral Instruction in the New Testament."
        Pp. 37–54 in *Women Hold Up Half the Sky: Women in the Church in South-
        ern Africa.* Ed. Denise Ackermann, Jonathan A. Draper, and Emma
        Mashinini. Pietermaritzburg: Cluster.

Du Toit, Andrie B.
1992   "Alienation and Re-identification as Pragmatic Strategies in Galatians."
        Neot 26:279–95.

Friedman, Roger
1996   "A New SA—But Women Still Second Class Citizens." *The Argus,* Jan. 8,
        1996:15.

Hartin, Patrick J.
1994   "Ethics and the New Testament: How Do We Get from There to Here?"
        Pp. 511–25 in *The Relevance of Theology for the 1990s.* Ed. Johann Mouton
        and Bernard Lategan. Pretoria: HSRC.

Hays, Richard B.
1989   *Echoes of Scripture in the Letters of Paul.* New Haven: Yale University
        Press.

1990   "Scripture-Shaped Community: The Problem of Method in New Testa-
        ment Ethics." *Int* 44:42–55.

Hendrix, Holland
1988   "On the Form and Ethos of Ephesians." *USQR* 42:3–15.

Johnson, Luke T.
1986   *The Writings of the New Testament: An Interpretation.* Philadelphia:
        Fortress.

Kirby, John C.
1968   *Ephesians: Baptism and Pentecost. An Inquiry into the Structure and Purpose of the Epistle to the Ephesians.* London: SPCK.

Lategan, Bernard C.
1985   "Reference: Reception, Redescription and Reality." Pp. 67–93 in *Text and Reality: Aspects of Reference in Biblical Texts.* Bernard C. Lategan and Willem S. Vorster. Philadelphia: Fortress.

1989   "Introduction: Coming to Grips with the Reader." *Semeia* 48:3–17.

1992   "Hermeneutics." *ABD* 3:149–54.

1993   "Textual Space as Rhetorical Device." Pp. 397–408 in *Rhetoric and the New Testament: Essays from the 1992 Heidelberg Conference.* Ed. Stanley E. Porter and Thomas H. Olbricht. Sheffield: JSOT.

1994a   "Aspects of a Contextual Hermeneutics for South Africa." Pp. 17–30 in *The Relevance of Theology for the 1990s.* Ed. Johann Mouton and Bernard Lategan. Pretoria: HSRC.

1994b   "Revisiting Text and Reality." *Neot* 28:121–35.

1996   "Imagination and Transformation: Ricoeur and the Role of Imagination." *Scriptura* 58:213–32.

Lincoln, Andrew T.
1990   *Ephesians.* Dallas: Word.

Louw, Johannes P. and Eugene A. Nida, eds.
1989   *Greek-English Lexicon of the New Testament.* Vol 1. Cape Town: Bible Society of South Africa.

McFague, Sallie
1982   *Metaphorical Theology: Models of God in Religious Language.* Philadelphia: Fortress.

Meeks, Wayne A.
1983   *The First Urban Christians: The Social World of the Apostle Paul.* New Haven: Yale University Press.

1986   *The Moral World of the First Christians.* Philadelphia: Westminster.

1993   *The Origins of Christian Morality: The First Two Centuries.* New Haven: Yale University Press.

Mouton, Elna
1994   "Reading Ephesians Ethically: Criteria Towards a Renewed Identity Awareness?" *Neot* 28:359–77.

1995   *Reading a New Testament Document Ethically: Toward an Accountable Use of Scripture in Christian Ethics, Through Analysing the Transformative Poten-*

tial of the Ephesians Epistle. D.Th. diss., University of the Western Cape, Bellville.

Niebuhr, H. Richard
1941   *The Meaning of Revelation.* New York: MacMillan.

Olyan, Saul M.
1996   "Honor, Shame, and Covenant Relations in Ancient Israel and Its Environment." *JBL* 115:201–18.

Perdue, Leo G.
1990   "The Social Character of Paraenesis and Paraenetic Literature." *Semeia* 50:5–39.

Ricoeur, Paul
1975   "Biblical Hermeneutics." *Semeia* 4:29–148.

1976   *Interpretation Theory: Discourse and the Surplus of Meaning.* Fort Worth: Texas Christian University Press.

1977   *The Rule of Metaphor: Multi-Disciplinary Studies of the Creation of Meaning in Language.* Trans. R. Czerny, K. McLaughlin, and J. Costello. Toronto: University of Toronto Press.

1980   *Essays on Biblical Interpretation.* Ed. L. S. Mudge. Philadelphia: Fortress.

Roberts, Johnnie H.
1991   *The Letter to the Ephesians.* Cape Town: Lux Verbi.

Sampley, J. Paul
1972   "Scripture and Tradition in the Community as Seen in Ephesians 4:25ff." *ST* 26:101–9.

Schnackenburg, Rudolf
1991   *The Epistle to the Ephesians.* Trans. H. Heron. Edinburgh: T. & T. Clark.

Schüssler Fiorenza, Elisabeth
1983   *In Memory of Her: A Feminist Theological Reconstruction of Christian Origins.* New York: Crossroad.

1988   "The Ethics of Biblical Interpretation: Decentering Biblical Scholarship." *JBL* 107:3–17.

Smit, Dirk J.
1994   "Morality and Individual Responsibility." *JTSA* 89:19–30.

Taylor, Mark K.
1990   *Remembering Esperanza: A Cultural-Political Theology for North American Praxis.* Maryknoll, NY: Orbis.

Thiselton, Anthony C.
1992   *New Horizons in Hermeneutics: The Theory and Practice of Transforming Biblical Reading.* Grand Rapids: Zondervan.

Turner, Victor
1974   *Dramas, Fields, and Metaphors: Symbolic Action in Human Society.* Ithaca: Cornell University Press.

Van Gennep, Arnold
1960   *The Rites of Passage.* Trans. M. B. Vizedom and G. L. Caffee. London: Routledge & Kegan Paul.

Van Huyssteen, Wentzel
1987   *The Realism of the Text: A Perspective on Biblical Authority.* Pretoria: UNISA.

Verhey, Allen
1984   *The Great Reversal: Ethics and the New Testament.* Grand Rapids: Wm. B. Eerdmans.

Vorster, Johannes N.
1990   "Toward an Interactional Model for the Analysis of Letters." *Neot* 24: 107–30.

Vorster, Willem S.
1989   "The Reader in the Text: Narrative Material." *Semeia* 48:21–39.

A NORTH AMERICAN PERSPECTIVE

Antoinette Clark Wire
San Francisco Theological Seminary

These essays show how much the experience of Asian, African, and Latin American women today can inform our understanding of the Bible and the world we live in. But the essays also show the struggles most women in the world must undergo to make this book their own. Because the Bible has been used to serve imperial and patriarchal agendas so successfully, it seems an unlikely text for women emerging from oppression. But for the same reason it appears to be a crucial text, both because its power requires its reinterpretation, and because this reinterpretation uncovers the kind of stories, prophecies, and confessions that are keeping women going in the struggle. Some essays here have focused more on exposing patriarchal structures then and now, whereas others are busy retrieving what is liberating and showing its centrality in the tradition. Apparently it is both "a time to tear down" and "a time to plant." These essays tell me that the deep plow's turning over the soil and the careful tending of fragile plants will go on simultaneously and for some time until new gardens of biblical interpretation are well established across the globe.

Though I will focus on the New Testament articles, let me mention how revealing I found the work on the Hebrew scriptures. Each person found in her own cultural experience special access to a biblical text that brought it to life while it illuminated her situation today. Women's traditional practices in relations of mothers-in-law and daughters-in-law, women's household economy, and standing in for each other in barrenness—hardly experienced in long-industrialized societies—turn out to be crucial in understanding these texts. At the same time the writers recognize patriarchal structures in the texts and in traditional societies today and wrestle with how to cultivate what is good without becoming servants in male-centered worlds. In one essay a special access to stories in Judges comes from the blatant violence that women in occupied countries still experience. Here it was especially clear that new biblical interpretations are only one means toward the primary task of overcoming militarism and male domination today.

I found the New Testament articles raising three key questions in biblical interpretation. How do we hear again the stories of the Near Eastern women at the generating point of our religious tradition? How are we to deal with biblical authors who have shaped these stories for their purposes? And can the New Testament help us participate in naming and changing our social worlds today? Though all the authors range across these questions, I will take up with each issue the two articles that seemed to make the greatest contribution in that area.

Hearing the Near Eastern women at the generating point of our tradition is most clear when Ranjini Rebera tells about Asian women reading Mary and Martha's story and when Malika Sibeko and Beverley Haddad describe South African women reading the hemorrhaging woman's story. Both essays stress the need for the stories to be interpreted by the women in local communities, not by others for them, nor in mixed groups with outsiders or men where people often restrict themselves to churchly or humorous readings. When Sibeko and Haddad show how women in Amawoti outside Durban zero in on church restrictions of menstruating women, we see that what the Bible has bound through a church's restrictive readings it can also set free—if women hear and evaluate its stories among themselves.

Rebera tells how in similar Asian settings a local storyteller can set up the story of Mary and Martha to highlight certain cultural issues, such as relations among sisters or with male confidants, so as to raise for discussion the real-life issues that come up for women of faith. She argues that Asian women have a long practice of oral storytelling and hearing by which they shape the traditions that guide their lives. So biblical women who did this can be brought in "side by side with Asian women" for consultation rather than prescription. Though such use of the Bible has been disparaged in Western academic scholarship, I consider that the recovery and hearing of women's stories will be at the foundation of future biblical scholarship. When we learn to respect the oral generators of our tradition, read the texts to hear them and appreciate the authors for preserving and elaborating their work, then we will conceive the synoptic problem and Christology and ethics in new ways more faithful both to the tradition and to ourselves.[1] Rebera's comment that an Asian woman puzzled how Luke heard Mary and Martha's story because they surely would not have told it outside the family suggests that women still active in oral story-telling may be essential as well in the difficult task of reconstructing who first told the biblical stories, to whom, and on what occasions.

But in our time when gospels and letters are read with all eyes on the evangelist's theology or the writer's artistry, it remains a challenge to shift the focus to the stories of the marginalized and their many women pro-

---

[1] See the work produced by the Programme for Theology and Culture in Asia's research projects titled "Story Theology in Religions and Cultures" and "Women in Society and Culture" (PTCA, P. O. Box 73598, Kowloon Central Post Office, Hong Kong). On biblical stories as oral story see Dewey and my forthcoming *Holy Lives, Holy Deaths: A Close Hearing of Early Jewish and Christian Story Tellers.*

tagonists. These essays suggest who it is that may make this shift and point scholarship in a new direction. Both Jean Kim's "ethical reading" of the Samaritan woman and Leticia Guardiola-Sáenz's "cultural reading" of the Canaanite woman charge the gospel authors and their scholarly readers with victimizing the foreign women portrayed. These two critics, applying the same new tools many of us are now using, come to this recognition through their own experience as outsiders in a dominant culture that dispossesses them by its ideology of chosenness and superiority. They defend their specific conclusions with careful exegesis I do not need to repeat. I want to ask how it is that they bring off the shift from privileging the text and its writer to honoring the story character and the reader's parallel experience.

There are points where they unravel the redaction of the author to find the story. Kim shows that John has interrupted the account of the woman sowing seed among the Samaritans to validate the disciples as its harvesters. And Guardiola-Sáenz sees Matthew taking Mark's story of Jesus going to a foreign place and turning the woman into a foreign intruder among Jesus' people. But this traditional approach of peeling off literary accretions is not the primary method used to hear either story.

Their major critical approach is to hear the cultural interests of the story character where they conflict with the interests of the author, whether, as Kim says, the author's irony begins a disruption that it cannot stop, or whether, as Guardiola-Sáenz (12) puts it, "the character escapes from his hands in search of a new author who can understand and respect her identity as the socially and culturally Other that she is." The biblical woman becomes in these readers' work a representative of the victimized Other today. She not only gets what she wants, as the gospel writers already concede, but she vindicates herself beyond the confines of the writer's story. Could we say: this is a woman *sin fronteras* reclaiming her share of the bread, one who knows why she has had five husbands and is not about to marry like that again. Thanks to her liberation through cultural and ethical readings of those who know her story first-hand, this woman is at work getting restitution. It sounds as though it depends on us who respond to her story whether her prophetic judgment presages our destruction, or whether it causes us to wake up, repent, and support the difficult work of restitution by learning to eat bread and drink water together as one humanity of multiple Others.

I will risk asking these critics if they might take their work a step further and explicitly claim the woman's story as the measure of the gospel. Could the Gospel writers, whom recent scholarship lauds for defining Jesus' identity and redefining the chosen people, have also achieved something else more important? They do transmit in however convoluted a way the encounters of women and Jesus, as Kinukawa puts. They reveal to some of us that Jesus is not top dog but is living water for those who claim it and pass it on.

He is not the assurance of the chosen but is a perhaps reluctant conceder of healings won by wise women providing for their own. Or is now not the time for Christology? Or is a more radical reconception of it needed? I do think many women are waiting to hear from you the upshot of the good news as you see it for our Christian faith.

This leaves two studies that interpret texts in light of a comprehensive view of present social settings. Musa Dube's post-colonial feminist interpretation from Botswana could have been considered with the above two essays, in that it reads certain texts in Matthew and John in tension with these authors. Yet because it focuses not on one woman but on the systemic crisis in a post-colonial world, I take it up as a parallel to Elna Mouton's study of Ephesians in a time of South Africa's transition. The textual work in the two cases is quite different, because Dube ranges across the New Testament to show how imperial settings stamped its ideology, whereas Mouton finds in the short letter of Ephesians metaphors for a time of transition.

The strength of Mouton's essay I see to be her careful work on the entire text of Ephesians in light of her social setting, making hers the only essay in this collection that takes the writer's complete statement as the key to understanding each part of it. This may be because the other critics are working in texts that are composite, or at least are made up of traditional units adapted by the writer and susceptible to independent consideration, whereas she alone has focused on a letter. Or is it that the European roots which she and I share have provisioned some of us distinctively so that we do not experience as sharp a dissociation as others do from the author's patriarchal world? She argues that the writer of Ephesians depicts God as unrelentingly gracious and Christ as head of the church through his love shown on the cross, so that husbands as well as wives are given this model of love and submission to each other, redefining the patriarchal relations otherwise intended by household codes. More convincingly to me, she also argues that the writer of Ephesians is drawing Christian hearers through a time of liminal tension as they move from their former Gentile alienation into a hoped-for full unity with Jewish believers and empowerment in Christ. Mouton sees that this open-ended call challenges modern readers to move beyond the author's patriarchal language and create an inclusive language appropriate for the wholeness of all people in Christ.

Like Mouton, Dube also insists that the meaning of the canon is not closed. As Jesus sent out his disciples into a mission beyond the confines of the text, the story continues to be read and acted out by each generation. But Dube argues that an oppressive imperial reading has dominated the history of biblical interpretation and privileged colonizing groups who depict their economic exploitation and political subjugation in narratives about travelers with a universal mission to the savages, legitimating this as the Christian mission in the Gospels. She calls feminists to be led through our concerns with gender oppression to do post-colonial readings that unmask the full range of racial, economic, political and religious oppression, rather than collaborating in silence wherever our own privilege allows us this advantage. It is not for me who have never even traveled to southern Africa to adjudicate whether the two conceptions of the social world in these two essays— "in transition" and "post-colonial"—apply to two different countries or to two different vantage points on the same social reality. In the interests of moving toward the "difficult dialogues" that Dube calls for, I would encourage her to articulate further what she sees to be the necessary stages in a transition from a post-colonial life to liberating interdependence and tell us more about how the Bible can be read with profit on the way. And Mouton might want to reconsider the adequacy of Victor Turner's stages—from prosperous and stable *societas* to liminal disorientation to final reintegration—for the present transition in which so many have no memory of prosperity and seek liberation, not reintegration. Perhaps Dirk Smit's categories are more adequate if you include not only his homogeneous premodern world and his pluralistic modern world but also the intermediate stage of authoritarian institutions. In that stage many people live out of fear and only a few have reason to respect and internalize the moral standards applied to them. This could help us see that the transition to a world of responsibility is not the same for all and the process of getting there cannot be universalized.

It is a great lift to read these essays. In the years to come we are going to have biblical interpretation by women grounded in the hard realities of this world and pointing us toward a real hope to come. Let this be a challenge to us to support each other well so that these voices and others like them do change the shape of our discipline and our world.

WORKS CONSULTED

Dewey, Joanna
1993   "Jesus' Healings of Women: Conformity and Non-Conformity to Dominant Cultural Values as Clues for Historical Reconstruction." Pp. 178–93 in *Society of Biblical Literature 1993 Seminar Papers*. Atlanta: Scholars.

Kinukawa, Hisako
1996   *Women and Jesus in Mark from a Japanese Feminist Perspective*. Maryknoll, NY: Orbis.

Smit, Dirk J.
1994   "Morality and Individual Responsibility." *JTSA* 89:20.

THE INDIAN VOICE

Monica J. Melanchthon
Gurukul Lutheran Theological College

This collection of articles has proven that in the fascinating challenge of honest and authentic cross-cultural sharing, mutual enrichment is inevitable. For a long time this did not happen because much of biblical interpretation even in the Two-Thirds world has been too deeply formed in the western light, or under its shadow, to be able to initiate new steps in sharing or dialogue. But the new and upcoming forms and methods of biblical interpretation, especially in the Two-Thirds world, make necessary a new kind of sharing—sharing between the Two-Thirds world and the First-world, between contexts of the Two-Thirds world and the Third-World in First-World contexts. Precisely when the domination of the United States over the rest of the globe seems all the more natural than ever, it could be important for western scholarship, including biblical scholarship, and women to travel in search of perspectives that might escape them as citizens of the world's only superpower. More to the point, this is an opportunity for western feminists to consider what they might learn from women in distant places. If women scholars at both ends of the world struggle together with some of the kinds of questions that arise in this collection of articles, it could lead to a more viable and accountable feminist scholarship than just the usual claim to universal oppression of women or sisterhood which has not enabled us to achieve much.

I would therefore like to thank the editors for giving me this opportunity to add my voice to the many voices represented in this volume. I have chosen to respond to only three of the articles—Musa Dube's article, "Toward a Postcolonial Feminist Interpretation of the Bible," Malika Sibeko and Beverley Haddad's "Reading the Bible 'with' Women in Poor and Marginalized Communities in South Africa," and Madipoane Masenya's "Proverbs 31:10–31 in a South African Context: A Reading for the Liberation of African (Northern Sotho) Women." These have been selected primarily because there are similarities between the cultural contexts of these writers and my own which therefore enable me to make a somewhat informed response. Constraints of time and space hinder me from making a more specific response to the other essays, other than a few general comments.

Women in India live in a situation where the highest place has been accorded to the female in Indian religious and philosophical thought. The primordial One is conceived as a harmony of *purusha* (male) and *prakriti* (female). The concept of *ardhanariswara* describes the god-head as half female and half male. The *shakti* cult is centered in the superiority and destructive strength of the female. Rivers and streams, dawn and twilight, flowers and seasons, knowledge and music are conceived of as feminine.

But, as in other countries of the world, there is a great discrepancy between the idealized concept of women and the real-life situation in which Indian women find themselves. They are burdened with cumulative inequalities as a result of sociocultural and economic discriminatory practices which until not too long ago were taken for granted as if they were part of the immutable scheme of things established by nature. Women are denied equal access to opportunities for personal growth and social development in education, employment, marriage and the family, and professional and political life. Even those women who have overcome the obstacles to professional education are disadvantaged as women because of the difficulty of reconciling the competing and often incompatible demands of a professional career with culturally defined homemaking responsibilities. The woman is conceived of as ritually impure and expected to treat her husband as lord and master. She is to worship him, run his home, and bear children, especially sons. This is considered her duty.

Women's deteriorating economic and social situation is manifested in violent crimes against women, which have been steadily increasing over the years, irrespective of the social or economic status of women. The figures available from the Women's Protection Cell for 1993 and 1996 reveal a significant percent of increase in the three years, with harassment topping the list, followed by murder, rape, and dowry deaths. In this heavily populated country, which is supposedly democratic and secular, one's caste, religion, class, gender, and language determine whether one will receive justice. Laws come to the aid of very few, and least of all to women.

In the persistent and worsening crisis of the world capitalist system, the ruling classes (upper castes) have developed safety nets for themselves in the guise of GATT, WTO, IMF, WB, and SAP. Using these, the monocapitalists both within and outside the country extract and appropriate from the workers and peasants and women a large chunk of the country's surplus value, deplete natural resources, and abandon to women society's responsibility for reproducing, caring for, and nurturing humanity and creation.

Women are hit hardest in this situation, as they number more than male workers, and this is reflected in the growing feminization of poverty. Through the media, religion, and cultural institutions, women are domesticated to endure the reproductive responsibility while simultaneously the State withdraws subsidies to social and medical services. Extreme poverty is killing our children and our women, and forcing children and women into prostitution.

Though there is some movement towards change of traditional roles of women due to the impact of the secular women's movement, education, and westernization, we are still far from the ideal. The Church is a microcosm of the larger society and women are not treated very differently. The Christian scriptures have been used to legitimize the low status of women, and women's secondary role is explained as being divinely ordained. Women are therefore urged to be submissive and to live as per the prescriptions of the Bible. Christianity in India has therefore tended, "in fact, to be much more patriarchal than the surrounding culture in India because of its institutional, theological and doctrinal rigidity" (Gnanadason: 59).

Feminist theological thinking is viewed with much suspicion, often branded as western and unsuitable to the Indian context. "Feminist hermeneutics," "feminist theology," and "feminist interpretation of the Bible," therefore, still linger around the edges and have yet to penetrate and affect in a significant manner the circles of Indian Christian theology. But Indian feminist scholars have called for a rereading of the biblical text in "a scientific way informed by a commitment to women's liberation and to human liberation in general" (Dietrich: 31).

It is against this very briefly described backdrop of the Indian context that I shall respond to the papers.

I

Musa Dube proposes a new way, useful or rather necessary in biblical interpretation—a postcolonial hermeneutic for reading not only Christian scriptural texts but also other religious and canonical writings. It is important to try to understand the proposed hermeneutic and then to assess it. I am personally not well versed in feminist theory, nor am I very knowledgeable in postcolonial studies. But having been born in a one-time colony of the British, and having studied the history of colonial rule in India, the effects of the missionary movement on the Indian Church and the current effects of the global market on Indian economy and society, I agree with the hermeneutic and recognize the importance of being aware of the fact that biblical texts were born in an imperialist setting and have been unique in sponsoring imperialist agendas over different times and peoples, and that this needs to be integrated into our feminist reading for liberation (Dube: 16–17).

Dube proposes a hermeneutic that is structured around several pairs of binary oppositions—male/female, whiteness/color, colonizer/colonized, rich/poor, Christian/non-Christian—with an emphasis on the colonizer/colonized and gender as starting coordinates. The model she seems to be alluding to is one in which all these intersect in either a multi-axial or multi-dimensional geometrical field to provide the necessary perspective in our interpretation of the text. The framework is quite attractive, but I wonder if there might be problems of performance because of too many "axes." It needs to be borne in mind that not all these axes are equal or symmetrical, nor should we venture to consider them so. I find it hard to imagine how such a multidimensional hermeneutic works, and I am afraid that we may lose the purpose, meaning, or aim of the text through such a search (cf. John: 96).

I am not recommending that we therefore turn away from such a multidimensional theory, but rather that we be aware that the various coordinates suggested are not reducible concepts. They are each loaded with meaning, have taken on different connotations in different periods of history, and have different histories and political positions. Hence, an example of the hermeneutic demonstrated would have been very helpful in understanding it and assessing it.

My second point is probably indicative of my own bias and in a sense is also a personal dilemma. Biblical interpretation requires a perspective, a critical stance from a defined angle that questions the inevitability or desirability of particular gender, racial, class, or imperialist meanings. The impetus toward such a critique does not come necessarily from a method but rather from the political impulse of the scholar (Gordon: 855). This is precisely where my dilemma lies. I am a daughter of postcolonial India, and my social stance is inevitably shaped by my social location as a middle-class, educated and, hence, privileged citizen of India. My Indian provincial innocence and my identity as a Dalit has been to some extent lost due to my social location and my travels and study abroad. I take the presence of women in the circles that I move in for granted, when outside my circles women are fighting for basic survival. Even so, I have pushed myself in order to be included in a class where modernity has enabled me a space, while my traditional culture would have hindered me from experiencing my current sense of freedom from both gender and culture (to some extent at least). My education outside of India has created from me a "west/imperialism" that is both within me and outside of me, and within the structures in which I work. The question for me, therefore, is, "How do I free myself from the imperialist notions that are a part of me to discern them in the text that is before me?"

Third, I would like to emphasize, along with Dube, the need to pay attention to other religious texts. Christianity is a minority religion in most of the Asian countries, as in India. The Christian population is only about 2.8% of the total population. Over the last several years, Asian theologians are employing what is called "extra-textual hermeneutics," an attempt to go beyond the Christian scriptures and look at literary and nonliterary sources that are common to all the people of Asia (Sugirtharajah: 3), to discern their understanding of humanity and divinity. It is all the more necessary for women to employ this hermeneutic because women in a multireligious context such as Asia suffer from what S. J. Samartha calls "double bondage" (1986:106–7). They are under the control of Christian patriarchal interpretations and also that of other major religions which have shaped and formulated the culture, the values, and the ethics of the country. It is necessary in such a situation not only to bring out the patriarchal assumptions of one's own faith or religion, but also those of other surrounding and dominant religions, and find solutions in collaboration with women of other faiths.

II

I particularly enjoyed the essay by Malika Sibeko and Beverly Haddad. The communal method espoused in the method is significant because it emphasizes that biblical interpretation can be relevant only if the community as a whole can appropriate the meaning of the text. This is characteristic of a collectivist culture over against an individualist culture where religion is personalized. In India too, Bible study is always a group affair where all the participants who join in the discussion benefit from the insights shared by the other. Secondly, reading the Bible from the perspective of the poor and the marginalized is being increasingly stressed as probably the only way to read the text. It is even more significant that it is poor and marginalized women who do this, because in India the poorest of the poor, the "Dalits of the Dalits,"[1] are the women who suffer triple discrimination on account of their gender, class, and caste. Not only are they oppressed by the upper caste communities but also by the men within their own communities. Any relevant biblical study in India must be done from their perspective.

My comments on this essay are less on the method than on the interpretation and insights that have been shared by the Amawoti women of South Africa, particularly in regard to menstruation. Like most human cultures, the Indian culture too believed menstrual blood to possess the mysterious magic of creation. Because of its central position as holy, dreadful, and even sacred, many male ascetic thinkers showed fear of it. The laws of Manu said that if a man even approached a menstruating woman, he would lose his wisdom, energy, sight, strength, and vitality. Brahmans ruled that a man who lay with a menstruating woman must suffer a punishment a quarter as severe as the punishment for Brahmanicide, which was the worst crime a Brahman could imagine (Walker: 641).

---

1 "Dalit" is a term meaning crushed, split, torn, oppressed, or marginalized. The communities belonging to the so called untouchable caste groups call themselves "Dalits," in opposition to other names such as "harijans," "scheduled castes," "depressed classes," etc., given to them by others. The term is a descriptive one, for it unveils the plight of these people.

According to Hindu custom, menstruating women are impure and inauspicious. In orthodox households, their activities are restricted. Regarded as extremely impure and temporarily untouchable, they are forbidden to enter temples, to cook, or to come into contact with others. Even the sight of their person and the sound of their voice were to be avoided. But today it appears that in keeping with the current decline in religious taboo, abstention from activities during the menstrual flow is no longer as widely practiced as it was thirty years ago—although many women are still conscious of being impure during menstruation and of the potential for polluting, and hence keep away especially from religious places. Elsewhere, pragmatism has taken over.

The story of the woman with the issue of blood bears many similarities to the condition of Dalit women in India. Dalit women are not impure only when they menstruate, but all the time, by virtue of their birth in one of the so-called untouchable caste groups and hence are discriminated against and oppressed all through their lives and in all spheres of their lives—economic, political, religious, social, and cultural. This is very much like the woman in the story who must have suffered in like manner, but for twelve years. Her impure state may not have allowed her to function at all. She was an outcast for twelve years. One needs to speculate on the cause of her continuous flow. Was it just a physical malfunctioning due to an anomaly in her body, or was it caused by some form of physical abuse? One wonders! Dalit women are often the targets of brutal rape by upper-caste men during caste conflicts. Even otherwise, Dalit women have to make themselves available to them when called. In recent years, it has come to light that many Dalit women suffer from ailments in their reproductive systems due to continuous exposure to hazardous chemicals in the leather-tanning industry.[2]

I would like to share here the insight of a male Dalit theologian who writes that the faith of the woman was of a subversive nature and that only such faith can generate power. Though unclean and polluting, "she dared to pollute others in order to become clean. The irony of this subversive faith is that she wants to break the laws precisely through channels that were created to remind people of the law and seek its compliance" (Devasahayam: 32; cf. Num 15:37–41). He continues, "subversive faith dares to act when it appears feasible by daring the obstacles" (Devasahayam: 32–33). This reminded me of Leticia Guardiola-Saenz' treatment of Matt 15:21–22 from the perspective of borderless women. The faith exhibited by the Canaanite woman who fearlessly crossed both human and divine boundaries in order to gain life for her child was a subversive faith. So also the woman with the issue of blood who

---

2 Leather tanning is a task that has traditionally been assigned to the Dalits. Since it meant working with the carcasses of dead animals, it was considered to be polluting.

was confined always to the fringes of society, discriminated against and powerless, who crosses human boundaries of gender and purity in order that she may have life. She needed to take back some of that humanity which was denied her by the community through no fault of her own, and hence she risked touching Jesus. Women are called today to dare and to risk, to cross boundaries in faith.

A second insight: By asking the question, "Who touched me?" Jesus was seeking the identity of the individual who deliberately touched him, and then publicly declared her healed. He did not care to follow the conventional rules of purity when *with* the woman or even after he left her, but proceeded instead to heal Jairus' daughter. The woman would probably have preferred not to have been identified publicly, but Jesus did, and his reason for doing so was for the sake of the men around him, rather than the woman—to expose their sin against her. "This exposure of the mistakes of the oppressor was of functional value for the oppressed—it builds the self-confidence of the oppressed" (Devasahayam: 34–35). By exposing the bias of Jesus, the Canaanite woman in Matthew 15 was able to get him to see his own weakness as a Jewish male and was able to gain what she wanted (healing for her daughter), thereby giving her confidence and self-worth.

III

The Bible to a large extent portrays the woman in her primary role as daughter, wife, and mother, and hence the Church today also focuses on these roles in its preaching and pastoral theology. Paul and the pastoral epistles are quoted repeatedly and in abundance to assert that the male is the head of the woman, exhorting women to be chaste, obedient, and silent. The tendency here once again is to confine the woman to her role as housewife. In other words, these Christian laws and ethical statements tend to focus on marriage and family alone.

Herein lies my problem with Prov 31:10–31, for it also focuses on marriage and family. Madipoane Masenya has very rightly pointed out that the poem upholds the positive elements of the Northern Sotho cultural understanding of womanhood which was lost during the process of colonization and westernization. The ideals in the poem concur also with the Indian understanding of womanhood. But the Indian understanding does not end there. There is a lot of burden placed upon the woman. Not only is she responsible for maintaining the household but, as mentioned earlier, she has to treat her husband as lord and master and is responsible for the safety and destiny of her husband and his afterlife.

She needs to produce male children in order that the name of the family be maintained, but also for the sake of performing rituals to guarantee that his soul rests in peace. There are rituals and rites that the Hindu woman performs in the calendar year in order that her husband will stay healthy and alive, because the woman is blamed if her husband dies early. A widow is therefore inauspicious and shunned in case she brings bad luck on those who are still married and therefore auspicious. Hence, it is the silent prayer of many an Indian woman that she die before her husband.

Masenya also rightly claims that the qualities of the woman in the poem are ideals one should strive for, but "*it was an ideal based on certain expectations which society had about women*" (emphasis mine). The ideals are not articulated by women but men, and hence I see a problem, because these ideals serve the purposes of men. It is not that I am against the virtues exemplified in the text; they are good qualities to be emulated. But if the ideal woman is confined to only the home, what is the message that it conveys to women who do not want to be homemakers in the traditional sense of the term? The poem creates a dilemma for me, a tension between what is considered to be femininity versus feminism. Anything a woman does which will not fit into this ideal is therefore considered nonfeminine. A woman who does not like to cook, or who has not learned to sew, or make pickles, is not well acquainted with craftmaking, is somehow not woman enough. Conversely, a man who may do these things is not male enough.

By focusing on marriage and family, subjects such as education and women, women and public life, women's contribution to economic and cultural production, and women as self-reliant human beings tend to be narrowed down to their contribution as wife, mother, homemaker. All I am asking is that we do not restrict our notions of womanhood to such a narrow area as the home and family. We need to focus both within and outside of the Bible on women who have lived lives in their own right, married and unmarried, in order that we develop a wider perspective. Otherwise, we will end up isolating many modern women who choose not to follow the traditional path—marriage, children, etc.

IV

Encouragement, stimulation, and challenge flow from the papers included in this volume. It is encouraging to note that some of the essays such as those of Ranjini Rebera, Leticia Guardiola-Sáenz, and Elna Mouton, have gone beyond the woman in the home to seek alternative roles for women. We need to analyze more texts by employing the method of materialist history, studying the actual position of women in the line of production during the time in which the text was written or the statement made.

Other themes which women should continue to pay attention to are female sexuality, women and politics, women and creation, women's understanding of God, women's spirituality, women and violence, and women and interfaith issues, to name a few. But just reflecting on the issues is not sufficient. Even as we emphasize the need for developing new methods and hermeneutics to study some of these themes, we need to be conscious of the fact that hermeneutics alone will not yield the truth (Samartha: 47–48). We as readers and intepreters need to develop sensitivity to the text through discipline, through feeling, emotion, and faith. Only to such readers will the text unfold or evoke meaning beyond that which is explicitly stated. But we need to go even beyond just discovering the meaning and significance of the text. We need to ascertain courses of action, or rather the interpretation should provoke us to act in new and meaningful ways to bring about the liberation of women.

In India, when women read and study the Bible together, the text is read; then, through the personal sharing of stories or case studies similar to the story in the text, connections are made between the text and the experience of women in the form of a discussion. The study ends with plans for a definite course of action that needs to be undertaken. In other words, the study of the Bible should end not just with interpretation, but evoke action. Only then are we on our way toward liberation and making a contribution to the renewal of the Church and the liberation of society at large.

WORKS CONSULTED

Devasahayam, Vedanayagam
  1996   *Doing Dalit Theology in Biblical Key*. Delhi/Madras: ISPCK/Gurukul.

Dietrich, Gabriele
  1986   "The Origins of the Bible Revisited—Reconstructing Women's History."
          Pp. 31–48 in *Towards a Theology of Humanhood: Women's Perspectives*. Ed.
          Aruna Gnanadason. Delhi: ISPCK.

Gnanadason, Aruna
  1993   "Feminist Thelogy: An Indian Perspective." Pp. 59–70 in *Readings in Indian Christian Theology*. Vol. 1. Ed. R. S. Sugirtharajah and Cecil Hargreaves. ISPCK Guide 29. Delhi: ISPCK.

Gordon, Linda
  1990   "*Gender and the Politics of History* by J. W. Scott." *Signs* 15:853–58.

John, Mary E.
  1996   *Discrepant Dislocations: Feminism, Theory, and Postcolonial Histories*. Delhi: Oxford University Press.

Samartha, Stanley J.
  1986   "But If It Is a Daughter She Shall Live." Pp. 101–10 in *Towards a Theology of Humanhood: Women's Perspectives*. Ed. Aruna Gnanadason. Delhi: ISPCK.

1991   "The Asian Context: Sources and Trends." Pp. 36–49 in *Voices from the Margin: Interpreting the Bible in the Third World*. Ed. R. S. Sugirtharajah. London: SPCK.

Sugirtharajah, R. S.
1994   "Introduction." Pp. 1–8 in *Frontiers in Asian Christian Theology: Emerging Trends*. Maryknoll, NY: Orbis.

Walker, Barbara G.
1995   *The Women's Encyclopaedia of Myths and Secrets*. London: Pandora.

About "The Other" and "The This"

Ahida Cama Calderon and Mercedes García Bachmann
Lutheran Theological School at Chicago

Rather than a passive acceptance of propaganda, liberation implies the problematization of their situation in their concrete objective reality so that being critically aware of it, they can also act critically on it. (Freire: 97)

Introduction

This volume of *Semeia* wants to celebrate the different voices/faces/signs of "diversity" because it is in the different, *not opposite*, realities where humanity encounters the most radical call, which is to find its identity in the difference. Where there is diversity, each particular reality cannot be just identified as the "Other." For what does a term like "the other" imply? That there is a "this one," or "the this"? It sounds strange to us. But exactly because this number of *Semeia* is dedicated to women from different parts of the world whose mother tongue is not English, we—being part of them—allow ourselves to coin a few new terms to better explain what we consider to be a relevant issue here.

In Hegel's dialectics of master and slave, we find a paradigm to express what appears to be developing in the way we look at "the other" from the perspective of "the this." If diversity is trying to find an identity based on this model ("this" and "the other"), it is bound to fail. A platform of dialogue cannot be reached if there can only be masters when there are slaves; or if there can only be orthodoxy when defined against heterodoxy; or if there can only be "chosen people" when somebody sets the borders of those who are lô-`ammî ("Not-my-people," Hos 1:9).

The "different" ways of reading the biblical text are what is at stake here. As a matter of fact, the religious experience of women still represents an unsolved issue in biblical studies. There is not enough evidence, or worse, there is no evidence at all to place their religious experience within the available categories. They either belong to the non-official religion, if we accept to look at them within the "generally accepted"(?) two *layers* of religion (Van der Toorn: 142–43), or their religious life takes a distinct form, as in the model described by Susan Sered (87) where the male- and the female-oriented religions are two religious *systems* in interaction with each other.

Women from Africa, Asia and Latin America offer in this volume a variety of readings of the biblical text, readings from/in/for their own reality.

For this response then we have decided to come to the same table to listen to our sisters' voices, to share what we have in common, and to learn how we, as women, can critically approach our own realities.

Before engaging in this dialogue, we would like to introduce ourselves. Ahida is a Roman Catholic, Peruvian, lay woman; Mercedes is a Lutheran minister from Argentina. We are both Old Testament graduate students at the Lutheran School of Theology at Chicago. What we have in common is that both of us have been professionally trained in reading the Bible, we come from the same region of the world, and we both share at the present time a considerable degree of freedom to speak out our beliefs. Yet our different countries, religious backgrounds, and undergraduate training have marked us in different ways, a fact that became obvious as we discussed our reactions to the papers. Our reading, understanding, and interpretation of these articles is consciously made from the following positions: (1) from our Latin American continent (therefore, suffering the imposition of a Neo-Liberal economic model, and witnessing its tremendous injustices); (2) from our position as minority in being Evangelical/Roman Catholic women in a male-oriented and male-dominated continent and Churches (and as such, having voices that remain unheard and having no access to decision-making structures); and yet, (3) from the position of the few privileged to have acquired an academic education (and thus, already far from the many women who read the Bible "only" from their experiences and often mediated by what the "religious experts" tell them is right).

This response is divided into two parts. The first deals with some of the characteristics we thought were common to most of the articles in this volume. In the second, we enter into the dialogue in this volume as participants from Latin America, engaging the articles from Africa and Asia, and particularly those focused on passages from the Old Testament.

I. Common Elements and Issues

It is not by chance that the first third of this response has dealt with ourselves and our beliefs. In fact, it mirrors what the vast majority of articles in this volume has chosen to do, namely, to make explicit the background of the writer as well as the readers with whom or from whom they have learned to read the Bible with new eyes. Rather than pretend objectivity, women theologians from Asia, Africa, and Latin America are being bold about who they are, where they come from, and from which context they read the Bible. Sometimes this created a feeling of impatience in us "trained exegetes." Yet, it is part of what it means to be theologians from the (Other?) Two-Thirds of the world, and of what it means to read after having a cross-cultural experience.

A second general fact worth highlighting in these papers is the resistance to romanticizing the victim. Although to a lesser degree than many of the people of our countries, women writing in this volume have shared in what it means to be a victim. As women, as poor, as racial, cultural or religious minorities, in apartheid or totalitarian governments, or in countries torn by war, women have suffered both oppression and injustice—and the humiliation of being coerced into a romantic view that denies us any right of reclamation. Like ourselves, the women of the Bible claim their right to be heard with new ears and open minds, and with hearts ready for conversion.

Women are depicted in some very well-known stories as "the 'humbled dog'" or "as the first fruit of the mission to the Gentiles, the pagan who needs to be redeemed" (the Canaanite woman; Guardiola-Sáenz, p. 70); or as "an icon for home-making and serving, within the life of the church" (Martha; Rebera, p. 99); or as the woman with an unethical life (who had five husbands and lives now with a "boy-friend"!) through whose dialogue "Jesus broke ethnic, religious, gender, and moral barriers" (Kim, p. 110); or the woman without a child, who even when married, becomes an adult only when she conceives (Mbuwayesango, p. 28). All these women here resist victimization and stand as "the Other" to the system (there is no diversity here!), claiming rights to a dignified life.

A third general comment refers to the articles that take the class factor into consideration. Class is not the only clue to understanding a text. We, Latin American theologians, however, emphasize this factor, because we understand that it permeates relations as much as sexism or racism do. But it is not only Latin American theologians that make the connection explicit. For instance, Madipoane Masenya points out that "African women thus know the inter-relatedness of these factors" (p. 56)—i.e., racism, classism, sexism, and those elements of the local culture (in her case, African) which contribute to the people's oppression. People without a high education know of this inter-relatedness "in the flesh," out of daily experiences and in their struggle for survival and for hope, while other people are able to articulate this struggle through political, sociological, theological terms. The two approaches can complement each other.

II. DIALOGUE WITH CONTRIBUTORS FROM AFRICA AND ASIA

Africa. Looking first at Mbuwayesango's article, we ask the following questions: What does the story of Hagar and Sarah tell us when we look at it from the perspective of their class locations? Why is allegiance to one's own class (Sarah to Abraham) more important than women's solidarity (Sarah and Hagar over against the male's need to have a son)? Mbuwayesango's comparison with the Ndebele and Shona contexts brings to the biblical story consideration of household and clan negotiations that we miss in the text.[1] However, coming from an urban, non-African context, it is hard for us to draw more specific comparisons. Does the class factor, which is important in the biblical story (Hagar and Sarah are *not* equals), play a role in the Ndebele or Shona societies? We do not know, but this could be another angle to look at it.

Turning now to Masenya's article, we ask: How do we read the "woman of worth" in Proverbs 31 when we do not belong to a social class that considers women worthy when they manage their household for the sake of a husband's honor "at the gates," or when women are single parents, or finally when women belong to those poor or servants that the "woman of worth" helps? And what kind of helping hand does she bring? Is it intended to change the system at all? Is it a palliative solution for the moment? Questions like these come out of the articles, as new windows open and challenge us to ask more questions about the texts.

Asia. Julie Chu emphasizes the importance of a partnership relation between women, in this particular case, between mother-in-law and daughter-in-law. Using the book of Ruth, Chu approaches a particular problematic situation of everyday life in Taiwan—the rivalry between these two women. The partnership relation between mother-in-law and daughter-in-law is almost absent there. The reason is because Taiwanese women *believe* that they "are made for men, either for being a wife or for being a mother" (Chu, p. 47). In trying to achieve their "imposed" roles as women in this society, their struggle for identity and unity as humans had been taken away. So this is not only a problem to be aware of, but a situation that requires critical reflection and action. To build a feminist consciousness and to recover the value of women we need to start from the grass-roots, that is, the everyday life.This is no small problem when there is abuse, violence, or oppression involved, especially, when this is "in every way" condoned by the structural protection of a patriarchal system.

Yani Yoo illustrates the violent face of that system in the horrendous criminal acts done against Korean "comfort women," and *a fortiori* against every woman. Yoo presents a biblical reading of Judges 19–21 that ironically cries out for justice—ironically because this passage in the book of Judges shows that the abuse of women is accepted as part of a war. How is one to understand or interpret such a biblical passage when real violence is being done to your own people today? Although in the biblical text we may find evidence of violence against women in the context of war, this does not justify it, in our view; there cannot be a romantic way to describe it. Violence is

---

1 See the abstract to her article (Mbuwayesango, p. 27): "In the Genesis narratives, Sarah is presented without any help from her kin, while in the Ndebele and Shona societies, the problem of a woman's barrenness is solved by her kin group and not by her alone."

violence no matter from what angle we look at it. Just to speak out about the Korean women's *han* will never heal the suffering that these women went through. However, Yoo's reading offers a final resolution: there is a way in which the biblical text can be interpreted, and that is in the appropriation of this text to say that the stories of the Korean women are not justified by the biblical text. On the contrary, what we have in the biblical text is clearly an "injustice" done to women, and therefore it is also an injustice today. Appropriation means to move beyond reflection and lamentation over what had been done; it means not to let it happen again.

FINAL COMMENTS

We have tried to see through the writers' eyes, and in many instances we have found ourselves sharing their view and being on their side. We tried not to be "the other," neither to be "the this" in our readings. This cross-cultural dialogue united us in the same language—a language of validity claims articulated with living words, although (or perhaps because) it also reflected our diversity. In this dialogue we are aware of the vantage point on which we stand (especially when trying to read the texts "with" the non-specialized woman); at the same time, as Freire taught us, we try to problematize the situation in order to bring forth changes.

Interpretation is not just understanding, but a discourse that leads us to appropriate our reality critically. The richness of contextualization takes priority over text-critical research. It is a valid way of reading the biblical text, isn't it?

WORKS CONSULTED

Freire, Paulo
    1989   *Education for Critical Consciousness*. New York: Continuum. [1973].

Sered, Susan Starr
    1992   *Women as Ritual Experts. The Religious Lives of Elderly Jewish Women in Jerusalem*. New York and Oxford: Oxford University Press.

Van der Toorn, Karel
    1994   *From Her Cradle to Her Grave. The Role of Religion in the Life of the Israelite and the Babylonian Woman*. Sheffield: Academic.

Printed in the United States
154583LV00002B/67/A

9 781589 831858